ACE THE
HALF

**RUN YOUR BEST HALF MARATHON,
GET IN SHAPE, AND FINALLY TICK
"FINISH THE RACE" OFF YOUR BUCKET LIST**

BY BEVERLY ASANTE PUSCHMANN

The Utterbloom Company LLC
Publishing Services provided by Paper Raven Books LLC

First Printing, 2022

Paperback: 978-3-9525639-0-8
Hardback: 978-3-9525639-1-5

ABOUT THE AUTHOR

As a former competitive high school and university athlete turned couch potato, who is now back on track as a half marathon runner, **Beverly Asante Puschmann**, a Certified Distance Running Coach and Certified Nutrition Coach, has walked (or rather: run!) the talk. She has researched everything you need to know to successfully run a half marathon—and compiled it for you in this book. Let the fun begin!

DEDICATION

*To my husband Florian and my best friend
Paz for keeping me inspired to write
and focused on getting to the finish line.*

*And to my son Luis, who will hopefully
run a half marathon one day!*

FREE BONUS

Would you like the AUDIOBOOK
of this book for FREE?

Available for FREE here:
ilovetorunandrace.com/acethehalfbonus

TABLE OF CONTENTS

MY LIFE AS A RUNNER

RUNNING FROM THE GET-GO

As a child, I was always the smallest and skinniest in my class, but the other kids respected me because I could run faster than nearly all of them. Sometimes they would tease me just to get me to chase them and to see if they could get away from me.

When I was in third grade, our sports teacher would take us out to a field each week to run. Most of the other kids took this as a social session and paired up with their friends to jog and chat. For me, it was competition time! I always tried to get to the finish line first. There was only one boy in our class of about 20 children that I could never beat.

The same year, our teacher announced that there would be a race against children from other schools. Excitedly, I signed up. My mother was psyched, too. She spent a whole Saturday afternoon going through town with me trying to find the right shoes. It wasn't easy because somehow, my feet were exactly in between shoe sizes. She took a leap of faith and ordered a pair of Nike Air Max—and they fit! I was ready for the race.

To get there, we took a three-hour bus ride, which was a challenge for me because I got motion sick in buses back then. When we arrived, I felt nervous but also pumped. The race was on a grassy field with some hills. I remember the grass being slippery and the weather gloomy.

My tactic was to break out of the pack fast to get to the front. I don't remember how long the race was, but it was somewhere in the range of one to two miles. By the middle of the race, I was still at the front, but there was a girl nipping at my heels.

I kept going, determined to win. And win I did. My mother was so proud she hung the medal up on the wall in our hallway.

In fourth grade, the sports teacher announced another cross-country race. I looked forward to it and kept telling everyone that I had won the race last year.

At some point, one of the teachers said to me, "You know, just because you won last year doesn't mean you will win this year."

I secretly thought to myself, *that's true, but you wait and see!* It was the first time it dawned on me that I was going to have to defend my title, and I was determined to fight for it.

This race was on home turf, exactly on the route that we had been training on, and I won again.

GETTING SERIOUS

From that time on, I continued as a competitive runner all the way through high school and then college. When

I recently dug out my medal box, I counted 27 medals that I won from third through 12th grade in cross-country and track-and-field (1500 m, 800 m, 600 m, 400 m), long jump, and high jump.

I also set two league records in the 1,500 m, the second one breaking my own previous record. Actually, the alumni office recently contacted me—apparently, I still hold the 800 m record 24 years later!

By the time I reached my penultimate year of high school, I was super fit. In the spring semester, I ski-toured up Mont Blanc, the highest mountain in the Alps. The same semester, I also had the unique opportunity to race at the Scottish Islands Peaks Race with my school. Our school was only sending one team to compete. That meant I had to be one of the six fastest runners—male or female—to earn my spot on the team. I ran as hard as I could in practice, and I qualified. I was elated.

The Scottish Island Peaks Race is a three-day running-sailing race. You sail on a boat to three mountainous islands. Each mountain has to be mastered by a team of two students and one teacher. It was an incredible experience of teamwork and spirit. The mountain I ran was on the Isle of Jura, where we ran a little over 12 miles with about 3,000 feet of ascent and descent.

After high school, I went off to Duke University in North Carolina, where I competed on the track team. Duke being a NCAA Division I Varsity school, it was much more competitive than my high school league. Quite honestly, the first semester was a rude awaking. Adjusting to the new academic environment and training schedule was tough. I was not convinced my coaches thought I was there to stay. But I did not give up, and after the summer between my first and second year of college, all of a sudden, my coaches seemed to realize that I had potential and that I was willing to work very hard. Finally, they started noticing me!

We lifted weights three times a week, and my legs became so muscular that all my regular jeans started breaking at the seams! I was a muscle package with practically no fat on me. I even had a visible six-pack back then, which was unusual for a woman. (It was almost a bit scary.)

In the summer of my junior year, we went to the Eastern Collegiate Atlantic Conference (ECAC)—a nice achievement. We had dreams to go to the Penn Relays the year after.

I started strong into my senior year, with a solid and structured summer training behind me. We kept focusing on our 400 m relay training.

And then I came down with mononucleosis.

The disease (caused by a virus) took me out of my regular daily life for four months. I was sleeping 16 hours a day and had to leave college for the rest of the semester. Even at the commencement of what should have been my final semester, I was still struggling with tiredness and lethargy. I only went back a year later to finish college. My dreams of the Penn Relays were squashed. My collegiate running career was over.

Somehow, I knew that at that stage in my life, I did not have the discipline to keep running without a team after college. I was defeated. And I stopped running for a very long time.

IN THE RAT RACE

After graduation in 2002, I moved to Connecticut and started working in the IT department of an investment bank. Times were tough after the internet bubble had burst, and to keep your job, you had to work long hours. Running did not seem to be a priority, and neither were health and nutrition. Once, a friend came over and was hungry. I said I didn't have any food in my house. She did not believe me, so she looked in my fridge. Lo and behold, there was Swiss Gruyere cheese and orange juice and nothing else.

She looked at me and asked, "So what do you eat?"

I said, "Cheese and orange juice for dinner, and if I am bored of that, I go out for sushi."

After four years of living in Connecticut, I moved to Switzerland, still working for the investment bank. Soon, I also got married. Still, there did not seem to be any compelling reason to exercise, besides the fact that my new husband kept nagging me.

Looking back now, even though I did work a lot then, there would still have been OODLES of time to go running. It just didn't seem important at the time.

In 2011, our son was born, and life got even busier. At that stage, I was a consultant for a tech giant. The beginnings were tough. Keeping a work-life balance as an 80 % (part-time) consultant, a mom of an awesome but very spirited child, the wife of an equally awesome husband, and so many other things at once made time even more precious.

It was when my son was about three years old that I started to realize what a toll the situation was taking on me. I had not been taking care of myself very well. I was getting too little sleep and I was eating unhealthy food. My college six-pack was long gone—just flab in its place. It was time to do something about it.

BACK ON TRACK

For many years, my husband had kept trying to get me to run again. He had heard from my college friends how fit I had been and how fast I was. In the spring of 2014, I was in my mid-thirties and had been more or less sedentary for 13 years. Even though I still looked slim, I felt unfit and had developed an unhealthy muscle-fat body composition. For the first time in my life, my blood work showed that my cholesterol levels were on the rise, heading toward an undesirable zone. No wonder. I had been eating bacon-lettuce-tomato sandwiches for lunch every day for the last three months!

It was that spring that the Global Corporate Challenge (GCC) at work (now called Virgin Pulse Global Challenge) took place. It was a program to get office workers to walk at least 10,000 steps a day. (On average, office people walk 3,000 steps per day—way too little for a healthy human being.) It aims to entice people to lead a healthier life by providing information and a fun way to compete with and against your colleagues and teams at other companies.

The managing director of the account I was working on had requested several times that I join the challenge. I said "no" several times, but eventually gave in. Once I agreed, he made me captain of the team.

It just so happened that most of my team members were men who were at least ten years older than me, and most of them were half marathon or marathon runners—which meant most of them were super-competitive sportsmen.

We signed up for the GCC and were ranked in the top three for our company in our country right away, so we decided to become number one. To win, each of us had to find a way to accumulate more steps a day. So, I started walking home from work, 4 mi (6.5 km) over a big hill, in heels and a suit, sometimes even in the rain. It was all about the team spirit, and we had a whole lot of fun.

Then I challenged my teammates to take 50,000 steps on a couple Saturdays. And that's how I decided to take up running again. I wanted to set an example for the team. I announced that I was going to run a half marathon, and this was where my journey started as a half marathon runner.

We did not win the GCC, but we came in a close second. And we were all a lot fitter afterwards than before.

I had no idea if I was really going to be able to run the half marathon, but somehow, I had to figure out a way to do it. I realized that I was so unfit, I couldn't even run for more than a few minutes without feeling my muscles burning and being completely out of breath.

Also, I was used to training in a team, with a coach, and running short and middle distances, so I did not know how to train for a long distance on my own. It was time to find out and put together a plan.

I started spending a lot of time researching everything from training plans to nutrition, equipment, weight loss, and health.

And all my research and experience as a runner has gone into this handy guide, so you can run your first or fastest half marathon too.

I became a half marathon runner when I was a married mom in my mid-thirties with a small child and a very demanding job. If I can do it, you can as well. Just use all this information that I've gathered for you and start training!

It's not always going to be easy. I didn't run all the half marathons I trained for, but I learned from each one, and each one was its own unique journey. And after so many years of running, not running, and then running again, I can tell you that when I run, I feel the best and the happiest, the most cognitively astute, fresh and fit, and I have the best sleep.

If this is what you want for your life, then I want to be your cheerleader and encourage you along each step of the way. Hearing a little about you and why you want to run a half marathon helps me help you. I read each email I get and can't wait to hear from you. Please share with me what inspires you to run your first or next half marathon by sending me an email at hello@ilovetorunandrace.com.

Once you do that, you can turn the page and start the exciting journey of your first half marathon! I can't wait to see you on the other side.

FINDING YOUR WHY

So, you've decided to run a half marathon. Congratulations! You've chosen a terrifically rewarding goal for any new, returning, or habitual runner. This book will help you with all the necessary preparation: training, equipment, fueling, recovery, and the all-important mental strength.

According to my research, the things runners fear most cluster around the following challenges:

- **Motivation:** How do I stay motivated or get unstuck? How do I not give up?
- **Mental Game:** How do I run the distance? How do I get rid of negative thoughts?
- **Nutrition:** How do I find my groove with nutrition? How should I fuel for my race?
- **Pacing and Speed:** How can I increase my pace and decrease my time?
- **Race Strategy:** How can I make sure my last miles are NOT hell? How do I calculate my race pace?

You've come to the right place. In this book, I will give you hands-on, tried-and-tested tips on how to prepare for a half marathon, whether it's your first or fourth. But before we get started, I'd like you to think about your **WHY**.

FINDING YOUR TOP MOTIVATOR

In his legendary TEDx talk "How Great Leaders Inspire Action," Simon Sinek developed the concept of purpose-driven action. "People don't buy what you do. They buy **why you're doing it**," he contends. And that's because our behavior isn't driven by our rational brain, but by our emotional brain.

Similarly, for our individual motivation, to reach a demanding goal, a strong WHY will go a long way. Otherwise, it's easy to get sidetracked, overwhelmed, or demotivated. Worst case: you quit.

If, on the other hand, you've found your WHY, it will add fuel to your engine and allow you to keep going even when the training gets harder. It will make you jump out of bed at 5:00 a.m., throw on your shoes, and RUN!

Are you feeling giddy and impatient because you want to get started with your training right away? That's okay. Why don't you go for a quick run right now to get it out of your system?

If you feel ready for your WHY now, go grab pen and paper.

Step 1

Give yourself 15 minutes and write down 30 reasons to run a half marathon. These may include health reasons, raising money for charity, proving to yourself that you can do it, or many others.

If you think of more than 30, even better! Keep going until the 15 minutes are over. Do not discriminate against any idea that comes up. If you don't have 30 by the end of the 15 minutes, keep adding five minutes until you have 30 items on your list.

Step 2

When you have your list of 30 items, circle your top 10 choices. Write them out on a separate list.

Step 3

Pick your top three from the list of the top ten.

Step 4

Decide which of the reasons is the most important to you. (You might combine reasons if they are very similar.) Make sure this reason is one you can connect to and evokes excitement for you. **This might just be the statement and the fuel you need to stay motivated.**

Step 5

Write a WHY statement in your own powerful words. Once you have written it out, read it to yourself and check if it resonates. If it doesn't, adjust the wording until it does. Can you feel it? Close your eyes and picture yourself running. Imagine you have reached whatever your personal top motivator is. Doesn't it feel awesome?

Here's my WHY statement for running a half marathon at the time of writing this book:

"When I run, my brain is in peak performance state."

Past experience had shown me that during times when I was running, I felt incredibly focused and driven. I wanted this feeling back. When I pictured myself reaching that state again, I felt giddy and excited all over. I wanted to get started right away!

Step 6

Write your WHY statement on a card and stick it in a prominent place, such as on the mirror in your bathroom or on your bedside table. **Review it every morning and every evening. Allow yourself to get excited with anticipation!**

SETTING YOUR GOAL

Now that you know your WHY, it's time to set a more specific goal and tell people about it. You might wonder why you should not keep this a secret—if you told everyone but ended up not running the race, that would be so embarrassing! Correct. That's exactly the point.

You don't want to give yourself any opportunity to renege on your commitment. Telling everyone about your goal and what you are doing to reach it will drive you to keep going. It will make it real. You are putting your social standing and your reputation on the line—you'd better achieve what you set out to do!

When I decided to run my first half marathon, I had barely done any sports during the previous 13 years and was not in good physical shape. To commit to the plan, I announced it to the whole team of my Global Corporate Challenge (GCC) at work. Now my professional credibility was on the line! I had turned it into a high stakes game. I wasn't 100 % sure if I would really be able to run a half marathon after being sedentary for so long, but somehow, I would have to find a way to do it.

My public commitment motivated me enough to train, come rain, shine, hail, or snow. While some of my colleagues would bail out whenever the weather was bad, my driving force was strong enough to pull through, no matter what.

Fast forward a couple of months: I ran my first half marathon in just over two hours. I was extremely happy for having taken on this challenge. Looking back, I was amazed that I could stick to my plan so diligently, despite juggling an engaging job, a family life with a small child, and running during my lunchtime hours.

Any response I got I utilized for additional motivation. If some people laugh at you or don't think you can do it, use that as your fuel to prove them wrong! If your friends and family are supportive and believe in you—great! They trust you can do it, so prove them right! Use that for strength when the going gets tough.

DECIDING ON YOUR SUPPORT SYSTEM

When I started running again in my mid-thirties, my husband (about the same age) started running again as well.

One time, he said, "When I was 20, I could run a 10k in 41 minutes."

I laughed at him and said, "I bet you won't run it under 45 minutes any time soon again. You are much older now!" He didn't answer, and I totally forgot about it. But in secret, he took it as a serious challenge and started training.

A couple of weeks before Christmas, he ran a 10k race in the city. At the finish line, he was beaming as he collected his banana and came over to where our son and I were waiting.

"You see, I did it!"

I thought to myself, *You did what?*

And he said, "You told me I was too old to finish a 10k in under 45 minutes, but I did!"

We had a good laugh together. It goes to show that you can use others' skepticism as wind in your sail to reach a goal.

If you feel comfortable with it, social media can be another great way to set yourself goals and publish updates on your progress.

On the other hand, be careful when choosing what goals you announce. For instance, I ran a 10k race as my preparatory race about a month before my first half marathon. And I told my husband the goal I wanted to achieve: 55 minutes. Now, one hour can be a sort of mental barrier for a first-time runner in the 10k world. I didn't think much of it at the time, but my husband got so excited that he told all our friends. Then my running watch broke down, the whole race was a disaster, and I was glad to finish it in an hour and a few minutes. It was a pretty good time for a 10k—but I'd missed my target. And since they'd all known about it, some of my friends unwittingly made some rather demotivating comments.

From that point onward, I decided to do it a bit differently: I would share a target time with my friends because people were curious, and it forced me to commit to a time. But secretly, I've got my own, real target, which nobody besides my husband and I know about. I want to stretch myself further than I am willing to wager publicly, so my private goal usually is more aggressive than the one I announce to the world.

This strategy has worked very well for me. I always set myself very ambitious (secret) stretch targets, so although I usually meet my publicly announced minimum target, I often fail to meet my personal goal. This method forces me to push hard, so I always get a good result.

My husband now knows to hold me accountable for my secret goal without telling anyone else about it.

ADDITIONAL MOTIVATORS

Once you have found your WHY, you have made the biggest step in motivating yourself. Of course, there are also other things, like willpower and external factors, that can keep us going and sustain the excitement. For instance, some people like to run with **running buddies**. If you enjoy running with friends, consider training together sometimes or joining a group.

I like to stick to my workout schedule, so on days I run intervals, I'm usually on my own. But if it's important to you, I'm sure you can find people who don't mind tagging along no matter what's on your training schedule for that day.

Many people find it easier when they're **sharing a commitment**, such as raising money for charity. So maybe you can motivate others to join you for a charity run.

Another way that I found extremely motivating was subscribing to the **Runner's World Newsletter** and being part of online running communities on Facebook. Not only do I find it informative, but it can add to the excitement: you feel you are part of the global running community.

Sharing your excitement with others by **sending short updates** to your running friends and support group can also be a great motivator.

A word of caution, though: not everybody is interested in running, and that's fine. Just be aware that some people who are not runners may not be as interested in regular running updates or might make comments that could demotivate you. Choose your audience selectively and share your running experiences with people who are genuinely interested and will put additional fuel into your motivation tank. If you share your new developments with the right persons, they tend to send encouraging messages back.

In summary:

- Finding your WHY can be crucial to your motivation and your mental game.
- Once you are certain about your WHY, you can start setting specific goals.
- Consider carefully if you want to announce your goals, when, how, and to who. Make a conscious effort to build a strong support system, including, for instance, family and friends, running buddies, or an online community.

WHY RUNNING
IS GOOD FOR YOU

GETTING HEALTHIER

If we look at the paintings in ancient caves, we don't see early humans sitting at desks, eating pizza, or drinking soda. Instead, they are hunting to provide food for their families and engaging in other physical activities. We've only started living a largely sedentary lifestyle and eating processed food a few decades ago. This is problematic because at the same time that we have become **less physically active**, our food has become more **calorie-dense** but **poorer in nutrients**—a deadly combination that has led us straight into a global obesity and diabetes epidemic along with other deadly, chronic diseases.

And ironically, the busier we get in our desk jobs, the more tempting it becomes to cut back on **exercise**. However, the opposite would be much more productive!

According to the World Health Organization (WHO), "Physical activity has **significant health benefits for hearts, bodies, and minds**." It can contribute to preventing and managing some of the main causes of death in Western countries, including **cardiovascular disease, hypertension, and stroke**, and many forms of **cancer and diabetes**. It helps to reduce symptoms of **depression and anxiety** and improves **muscular and cardiorespiratory fitness, bone health, and sleep**. A recent *New York Times* article also neatly summarizes research showing that regular exercise **boosts your immunity** against infectious diseases in the long run.

Even better: by moving our bodies, we enhance the health of our brains, too! According to research by David Linden, PhD and professor of neuroscience at the Johns Hopkins University School of Medicine, systematically engaging in cardiovascular exercise can stimulate the development of the vascular system and even neurons, as well as generally improve our brain performance and prevent cognitive decline. Who wouldn't want that?

I can certainly attest to the effects that running has on my own cognitive functions. When I started running again, I noticed that it became much easier for me to focus on my work and make good decisions. I also sleep much better during times when I run.

In short: running is a stepping stone toward a longer, healthier life!

FINDING MORE BALANCE IN LIFE

When times at work get stressful, I am reminded of my childhood pet hamster. Sometimes, he would run so fast that he would somersault in his running wheel!

It can feel that way in our busy lives, as well. If you work as a freelancer, you might have a bit more decision power over the pace of your wheel, while if you're working as an employee, your employer might decide the pace of your individual wheel. When you are holding on to the wheel for dear life as it spins out of control, you know your life is out of balance!

I like to think about how I can reach the ideal balance between work and life, especially when I see family, friends, or coworkers seemingly dedicating their whole life to their work.

When I started to run again, I had decided that I did not want to fall into that trap. And I had realized that personally, I would never regret doing whatever needed to be done to run a half marathon. On the contrary, what I would regret in the future was if I didn't follow my dream because I thought I didn't have the time for it. And running a half marathon was an achievement I really wanted under my belt. I knew that the training necessary to reach that goal would never fit perfectly into my schedule. So, the best time to start was today!

Before I started my training, it was hard to imagine how I would ever find an additional four to six hours every week for running. But because I was so driven by my WHY and my goal, I found ways to make it happen.

My strategy was to **structure my schedule in more detail than I had in the past**. I started timeboxing activities and training myself to be more efficient at certain tasks. I stopped obsessing over work already done and done well. And guess what: I kept delivering high-quality work, and my ability to concentrate has increased due to my training. Win-win for my employer and me!

Of course, that doesn't mean you have to spend the same amount of time on your training as me. It's completely up to you how much you can and want to invest in your training. You can certainly choose a lower-volume plan than I did. (I have devoted a whole chapter on training plans and how to find the most suitable version for yourself.) If you are lucky, a supportive partner may take on a bigger share of the domestic work or childcare while you are out on longer runs.

One promise I made to myself was that I would not take my training hours out of my sleeping hours. Sacrificing sleep would have been counterproductive in many ways, considering that when you are tired, you cannot work as efficiently and may make mistakes that will take you longer to reverse than if you had avoided them in the first place.

The Wellness Council of America nicely summarizes a study on the effects of sleep deprivation on productivity. Essentially, sleep deprived employees were about 1.9 times less productive than employees that got eight hours of sleep a night. The economic damage is enormous! Other studies show that mild sleep deprivation is as detrimental to your driving as is low-level alcohol intoxication.

To sum up: what seemed like a burden or at least a challenge at first turned out to be a significant gain in the long run: training required commitment, organization, and discipline, which led me to a more balanced life because it prompted me to establish a more deliberate, healthy schedule. I decided what my top priorities were and made up a plan based on those. Family and health (including exercise, sleep, and eating well) were at the top of the list. Having set these priorities, I scheduled sleep, family, and exercise in my schedule first and everything else around it.

Of course, friends and work also had a high priority, but in order to enjoy all that for many years to come, I would need optimal health.

MAKING NEW FRIENDS

When I took up running again, I started off on my own. As I began to tell friends and coworkers that I was training for a race, they responded with curiosity and sometimes even excitement.

"Oh, you are a runner?" they asked enthusiastically. It was at that point that a whole new world opened up for me.

I started to connect with other runners and found running mates for my lunchtime runs. In general, I like sticking with my training plan, which means that sometimes, my partners in crime wouldn't like to join me on some of my runs. On the other hand, there were runners who were willing to come along even on days when I did hill sprints. Even different levels of training didn't necessarily have to cause problems; for instance, what some runners might count as a recovery run would amount to a tempo run for me, but we could still run it together.

Running is also a great way to connect if you recently relocated or started a new job. Many towns, cities, and sports stores have running clubs or events where you can join for runs or clinics to meet fellow runners. I found networking with other runners motivating, even if I did not run with them. We would share our workout and race pictures and tell each other stories about our personal breakthroughs.

Being part of a community made my training more fun and helped me facing the difficult parts without throwing in the towel. It just helps you to stay on track.

RECHARGING IN NATURE

Part of the fun of training for me was that I spent more time in nature. The more I ran outdoors, the more I noticed the small things around me: colorful birds playing by the river, trees budding, the smell of the flowers in the fields… It's amazing how much you can experience on a five or 10k run! I also noticed how nature would draw me back to running when I was not motivated, particularly after phases where I had primarily been running in urban areas. And it was so relaxing!

As a 2010 Harvard Medical School Health Letter points out, being outside has measurable health benefits. For instance, you produce more vitamin D, which helps to "fight certain conditions, from osteoporosis and cancer to depression and heart attacks." Taking in more daylight will also help to improve your mood; the Harvard experts praise exercising in nature as the perfect combination to become healthier, happier, and more relaxed. Children with ADHD showed better concentration after spending time outside. And there are convincing studies to suggest that being in nature can help you heal faster after an injury or operation.

And there are so many other reasons to go running! Someone I know who travelled a lot told me that he loved to run at his destinations because it was a great way to get to know the places he travelled to. It gave him an immense sense of joy. He would simply tell his sports watch what distance he wanted to run, and it would suggest routes that other runners had already tested. It was like an extra bonus for going on a business trip that he always looked forward to.

In summary:

- There are so many reasons why running is good for you! It will help you to keep (or get) fit and healthy, it can improve your sleep, and it may help you to find a better work-life balance or to find new friends.
- Try to run in nature as much as you can because there are proven additional benefits, such as lower stress levels and better concentration.

EQUIPMENT

SHOES–YOUR MOST IMPORTANT INVESTMENT

To get started with running, you don't need a lot of equipment, but you should invest in a good pair of shoes. It took me a while to realize this.

When I took up running again in my thirties, I didn't give much thought to what I would need for my re-found hobby. I figured I would just pull out my 13-year-old running gear and only invest in a new pair of shoes. So I went to a sporting goods store at the mall and bought some shoes on sale. Yes, just a random sporting goods store, not even a running store! Big mistake...

I walked out all proud of my purchase. The next day, when I pulled out my shoes to go for a run, my colleague at work took one look at them and said, "You're not going to run in these, are you?"

"Why not?" I said.

"Because they aren't running shoes," he said. He was an ex-professional athlete, and when he explained to me how important good running shoes were to prevent injury, he quickly had me convinced.

You would not buy a dangerous car to drive your family around, right? So why would you choose to run in shoes that dramatically increase your chance of injury to one of the most important sets of limbs and joints in your body? You really want to protect them against the impact of your feet pounding on the ground with each step. And if your feet don't get the proper support, you could get some nasty lower limb injuries. If, on the other hand, your shoes are not made to run on asphalt, they may simply break.

So far, the best place I found to buy running shoes is in a **running specialty store**. On my first visit to the running store, I realized there was a whole science around running shoes! The good news is that modern running shoes can accommodate just about any foot.

YOUR FOOT TYPE

There are mainly three types of feet that work the ankle and foot differently when they strike the ground and roll differently while running: **flat feet, medium-arched feet, and high-arched feet.**

Consequently, there are three (main) types of shoes: motion-control shoes, stability shoes, and cushioned (also called cushioning) shoes.

1. **If you have flat feet, your feet will roll inwards when you step down.** This movement is called overpronation and causes your ankle to not absorb the shock effectively.

In this case, you will want to buy motion-control shoes, which will help against **overpronation**.

2. If, **like most runners, you have medium-arched feet, your feet will roll inward at about 15 degrees to absorb the shock of the strike in the most effective way.** Medium-arched feet are the most common type and the type associated with the least amount of injuries. For these type of feet, your best choice will be **stability shoes**, which allow normal pronation and shock absorption.

3. **If you have high-arched feet, they will roll inwards less than a medium-arched foot and cause the shock to be absorbed in one small area. This is called supination or underpronation.** With these type of feet, you will want to buy **cushioned shoes** to absorb the higher shock to the foot.

Every individual has their own idiosyncrasies and possible misalignments when it comes to their body and the way they run. However, today's running shoes can accommodate and compensate for most of these imbalances fairly well. It's important to have a basic understanding of foot types. However, don't worry too much about it but rather go to a specialized running store where they will help you to figure out what your foot type is and which kind of shoe is right for you.

FINDING YOUR RUNNING SHOES

I really recommend getting in-person advice to buy shoes rather than buying them off the internet (even if that would be cheaper). The advice and relationships you build with the staff at your local running store pay off over time. My first visit to the running store did not only teach me a lot about feet and shoes. I also learned about local races, local clubs, locally prominent runners, and much more.

Another place to buy sports equipment is at running fairs at races. There, you can get everything from shoes to clothes to recovery nutrition and running watches, frequently at discounted prices.

If you have the opportunity, visit a couple different dedicated running stores and get some advice on what fits your feet. Here are some indicators that you are getting good advice:

Your salesperson

- measures the **length and width** of your feet (or at least tests the shoe on your foot with their hand)
- asks you about the type of **terrain** you will run on
- asks you about your **mileage**
- asks you to run to see if you are a **front-, midfoot runner, or heel striker** and how you **pronate**
- asks you whether you use **orthotics**
- asks you where your running shoes usually **wear off first**
- asks you to **run in the shoes** you are about to buy

I walk out if the salesperson doesn't cover these basic points or doesn't seem to understand anything about running or running shoes.

Does the Shoe Fit Checklist

Here's a checklist that will help you decide if the shoe you found could be a good fit:

- ❑ there's **enough space at the front** for your foot that it won't touch when you run downhill
- ❑ there is **enough space** in your shoe in case your foot **swells** when you are on a long run
- ❑ the shoe is **neither too wide nor too narrow**
- ❑ the shoe is suitable for the **terrain** where you want to use it
- ❑ the shoe feels really **comfortable**
- ❑ you feel good about the **advice** you got in the store
- ❑ you feel good about the shoe and **motivated** to wear it to go running

ORTHOTICS

Some people, no matter what shoes they wear, will need **orthotics** to stay injury-free. Keep an eye out for the wear on your shoes and, more importantly, any aches or injuries you may have incurred before. If you observe the slightest trouble, I'd have it looked at. The best option I recommend is to visit a **podiatrist or orthotics specialist**.

They use specialized equipment to find the best solution for you. (Many running stores do orthotics as well, but I'd still prefer having them made by a podiatrist.)

If you already have orthotics, you must **bring these along when you are buying new shoes**. Otherwise, you might well find that the shoes simply don't work for you anymore once you put the orthotics in.

WEAR AND TEAR

Once you've used your running shoes a while, make it a habit to **turn them around** and check for signs of wear and tear every now and then. You can discuss with your trusted salesperson in the store when it is time to replace a running shoe. Usually, you should be able to get **300 to 500 mi** (480 to 800 km) out of a running shoe. However, it depends on many factors such as terrain, weather conditions, your average weekly mileage, your gait, and so on.

Don't stress too much about it or let yourself be tempted into overspending. If, however, you start feeling pain in your feet, knees, hips, or shins, it might be worth considering whether your shoes are ready for retirement. **Worn shoes can cause many different type of injuries in the lower part of the body.**

You can prolong the life expectancy of your running shoe by only using them for running, not for everyday activities or cross training. You can also rotate them if you own more than one pair or have different shoes for different terrains.

CLOTHING

The technology had advanced incredibly when I took up running again after my 13-year abstinence: running clothes wicked away moisture much more effectively, were much lighter, softer, and generally way more fun to run in. They even had pockets for keys and phones or a music player!

I once asked a salesperson in the store what the difference between running clothes and non-running sports clothing was.

She rubbed her index finger and thumb together and said, "It's hard to explain. The material is different. It just feels different when you run." At the time, I was irritated by this vague answer and decided to ignore her advice. So, I bought some gear that was labeled fitness. Another big mistake…

The main difference, as I've found out since, is that in a fitness studio you are not usually confronted with **temperatures in the 100s F (37 to 42 °C) and 90 % humidity**, as you are when running outside in the summer. I later realized that the dedicated running gear felt a lot drier and smoother on my skin at high temperatures.

Another reason to buy clothes meant for running: you usually get extra **pockets** for keys, credit cards, bus tickets, and a music player or phone, which you don't usually find on fitness clothing.

A **running store** would probably provide the best advice on running clothes, but **brand stores** can also be a good place to look, provided you stick with the clothing labeled "running."

Depending on where you live, you may need different running gear for different seasons. I tend to break my gear down into the following weather categories:

Warm Weather

short t-shirt
shorts
short socks

Spring & Fall Weather

long/short sleeves
3/4 pants or leggings
light, water-repellent jacket (if wet)
short socks

Cold Weather

long sleeves (merino wool if going for a long run)
long leggings
hat
gloves
light, water-repellent jacket (if wet)
long socks

I hardly ever wear more than this. If the weather in your location gets very cold, you may want to add **thermal undergarments** such as thermal leggings, a thermal shirt, etc. in very harsh conditions. Some people like keeping their neck and/or head warm using a BUFF® scarf or something similar, but keep in mind that **most runners tend to dress too warmly**. (I used to, too.)

You will have to experiment and find out what works for you. I have seen people running in shorts even when it was snowing outside. Other people wear what I would consider my cold weather gear when I am in shorts and a short-sleeved t-shirt.

The important thing to watch out for is that you are not too warmly dressed, particularly when you are racing. It's easy to underestimate, too, that during a race, you may run faster than in your training runs, and the weather conditions might vary from what you are used to as well. **You do not want to overheat** and risk discomfort or even a collapse during your half marathon.

A good rule of thumb: **when you go out, you should feel a bit cool at first; about five minutes into the run, you should feel good**. (Of course, if you are training in the Sahara, you are going to feel hot either way, but presumably, you will know what to wear in that weather.)

Last but not least—speaking of the Sahara—don't forget to.protect yourself from the sun (sunscreen, sun protection lip stick, hat or cap, etc.)!

RUNNING BELT

A running belt is a belt going around your waist or specialized kind of chest holster that allows you to carry nutrition and fluids with you when you go on long runs. It is a critical part of your refueling strategy. You might even decide to race with the belt if you have a sensitive stomach that can't tolerate the nutrition they provide at the race (see Fueling & Refueling). If you want to race with the belt, you will want to ensure that it is relatively lightweight.

SOCKS, UNDERWEAR, SPORTS BRA

There are many great materials used for sports socks and underwear nowadays. If you are just starting out as a runner, I suggest you simply shop around, get a feeling for what types of materials or brands you like and ask advice in a running or sports/outdoors store. The most important criteria are as follows: you should feel really comfortable, and they should fit well; they should not rub against your skin, or otherwise you could end up with painful skin irritations or blisters; and they should wick away sweat well. Make sure you tell the salesperson that you are going to use the clothes **for running (including outdoors)**. For instance, a **sports bra** will probably need to give you more **support** for running than one used for some other types of sports.

TRAINING WATCH

The last decade has seen a big shift in the training watch landscape. Where in the olden days, you had to connect your watch to your computer, it now synchronizes itself via your home Wi-Fi or phone. What used to be a watch might now have become a phone, activity tracker, or training smartwatch. (I will call whatever device you use a training watch.) Training watches today can tell you everything from your heart rate and pace to how to get home and what the weather is going to be like. They even show you your partner's text message letting you know that dinner is ready!

No doubt the development will continue rapidly, which is why, in addition to the information in this book, it's essential to talk to a specialist salesperson who can advise you on what device fits your situation best. Running stores or reputable sporting goods stores that carry training watches should be a good place for such a purchase. Just make sure that the salesperson is seriously knowledgeable about the training watches they sell. Also, www.dcrainmaker.com is a great resource for all kinds of gear, especially electronic equipment.

If you are just starting to run, you won't need a training watch right away because you will start out running at a conversational pace.

If you have been running without a training watch, you might wonder why you should suddenly change your ways. Here is my answer: because for high-quality half-marathon training, you need to be able to measure your training intensity. The training plans chapter will explain the different measuring methods, which will in turn influence your decision on which training watch to choose. You may decide to postpone that decision if you are already using a phone or activity tracker. In any case, if you are planning to invest in a (new) training watch, I recommend you read the chapter on training plans first.

If you already have training sensors or equipment from another sport such as cycling, then some of the decision is already made for you: you will probably want to choose a watch that's compatible with the sensors you already have and the measuring method for your training intensity that you are already used to and comfortable with.

Features

My recommendation is that you train with a watch that has **at least the following features**:

1. heart rate
2. pace
3. distance
4. time
5. lap (lap number and what time in a lap you are at)
   Nice to have, but **optional**:
6. power (see Training Plans chapter for the pros and cons of power measurement)

The first three features (heart rate, pace, and distance) need to have a reasonable degree of **accuracy**, e.g. if your pace changes, this should be reflected on your watch with a minimal delay. **The lap function needs to show you the**

time and distance for the current lap as well as heart rate, pace, and distance even if you need to scroll to a new page to see them.

Many watches offer way more features, not all of which are necessary to complete your workouts. However, I'm the kind of person who likes gadgets, so I opted for a watch that also tracks my **activity and recovery status** and lets me measure my **fitness**.

If you decide to train with your phone or activity tracker, you should ensure that you can connect a heart rate monitor chest strap. You want to have an accurate read of your heart rate. If you are thinking about using a watch without a chest strap (which measures your heart rate at the wrist), you should consider that at the time of writing, many of these watches were not very accurate. I suggest you research the accuracy of the wrist heart rate measurement very carefully and seek advice from a specialized salesperson. (For more information on heart rate measuring, see the Training Plans chapter.)

Apps

Most apps will give you the basics on your phone such as **pace, distance, and time,** and some of them will let you connect to sensors such as a **heart rate monitor or a foot pod** (to measure your **pace and cadence**).

Here are a few training apps that you might consider using to **record, track, analyze, or share your training efforts**:

- **Strava:** Many rankings rate Strava as the running app. It could be for you if you like to compete and to be "**social**" (online).

- **Runtastic:** If you are looking for an app with a **virtual coach** or integrated music, Runtastic offers this along with a host of **pre- and post-workout information** you might find useful.

- **Runkeeper:** Ideal for runners with a serious goal such as a half marathon. It pairs with many fitness devices and allows **GPS tracking** while also offering **training plans** in the app.

- **Map My Run:** A good choice if you do several types of activities and are looking for an app that connects with your sensors, connects with other apps, and offers you accurate pace indications.

One of the many things I love about running is the fact that you can do it almost anywhere, anytime, without needing much equipment or preparation. **The only thing I am adamant about is buying good running shoes.** Once you are getting more serious about your half marathon training, you will want to buy a training watch and other gear, but if you can't afford sophisticated equipment, don't let it keep you from running! You can always add what you need when you are sure you really need it. (It's easy to overspend in the first rush of excitement.)

However, if you have the means and enjoy cool gadgets and fancy equipment—go for it! It will make your running experience even more enjoyable.

In summary:

• Your running shoes will be your most important investment. Make sure to visit a specialized running store and get good advice by a trained salesperson. See to it that your shoes fit your foot type, the mileage, and the terrain you will be running in.

• Running clothes, as opposed to general fitness clothes, deal better with outside temperatures and offer pockets. The most important thing is to avoid overheating by dressing too warmly!

• Choose your training watch (and other measuring equipment you may need) AFTER you have chosen your training plan.

TRAINING

Before you get started, make sure you are ready to run. You don't want to jump up from the couch and start running 5k for the first time in your life—you would only set yourself up for disappointment and risk injury or other health issues. Be smart about it! Before starting any exercise program or training plan, ensure that you have had the necessary medical checks and your healthcare provider has given you the go-ahead to start training. If you have any pre-existing health conditions or have been injured before, this will be all the more important for you. This also gives you a baseline you can measure yourself against in the future. It might give you a huge kick of extra motivation to see certain aspects of your health improving over time! Training for and running a half marathon is great fun, but it may not be appropriate for everyone.

I highly recommend using a training plan to prepare for your half marathon race. A training plan gives you a structured system that indicates what type of workouts you should do on which days and at what intensity level. There are many good training plans out there, designed, tried, and tested by excellent professional coaches and trainers, so I won't waste your time coming up with my own version of a training plan. I will, however, tell you all you need to know to choose the right training plan for yourself, which is essential for your success and well-being.

WHY STRUCTURE MATTERS

If you are a person who loves measuring, planning, and a structured approach to pretty much everything, keep reading! You'll be very happy researching and choosing a training plan that guides you through the whole process of training for a half marathon. If you are a returning half marathon runner and you've picked up this book, it might well be because you have had some not-so-great experience with your training and preparation or your race results, so, again: choosing the right training plan could make a huge difference when preparing for your next race! Or you might loathe the whole planned and structured approach, considering yourself a person who prefers winging it. If that's the case, I hope you will keep reading and follow my advice, especially if you are new to half marathon running or running altogether.

There are many good reasons to use a well-thought-out and well-structured training plan. **First and foremost, you want to do all you can do to prevent injury.** I've been extremely lucky myself: I've rarely had any injury to speak of in my whole running career. But time and time again, I have seen other runners get extremely excited at the beginning of a running journey. As a result, they **increase their mileage too quickly or take too few rest days** and end up hurting themselves. (Common overuse injuries from ramping up mileage too fast are **iliotibial band (IT Band) syndrome and shin splints**, both highly unpleasant. You will find a link in the resource page in case you intend to dive deeper into these injuries and how to avoid them.)

A well-thought-out training plan will **increase the mileage gradually (i.e., no more than 10 to 15 % of your weekly mileage each week)** to avoid this type of injury.

PERIODIZATION AND BETTER TRAINING EFFECT

The way training elements are timed and structured in a training plan allows you to increase your speed and endurance to yield **maximum results. Not all intensity levels have the same training effect.** For example, a slow and easy run can help your body recover actively from a strenuous workout the day before, whereas a tempo run (advanced level) trains your body to clear lactic acid from your muscles. A training plan includes a training intensity for each workout to ensure that you do the workout at the intensity that has the correct long-term effect on your body.

A good training plan will also have **recovery weeks** in which you decrease your mileage significantly to allow your body to adjust before increasing the mileage again.

If you don't recover adequately, you risk **overtraining**— which means you break down tissue in your body faster than it can build it up. If you overtrain, you can lose a significant amount of time for an enforced break before you can recommence your training.

In addition to your training plan, it helps to structure all other important aspects of your well-being and fitness as a half marathon runner, too, including nutrition, hydration, adequate sleep, training, and equipment (see the respective chapters).

One of the most important things a training plan will help you with is called **periodization**. This means that a good training plan will guide you through different phases of training, leading to your ultimate performance peak by the time you are running your half marathon. (If you are a repeat half marathon runner, chances are you are studying this book because you were not happy with your former training results, either because the race was unnecessarily hard and unpleasant for you or because you know you can run faster—but need a better way to get to the results you're craving.)

The base of the periodization pyramid starts you off with running up to 500 miles at conversational pace, i.e., a pace where you can hold a conversation without sounding choppy because you are getting out of breath. This will be the most significant segment, in terms of volume and time. The second phase builds up strength. This phase will usually include tempo runs, fartleks, and running uphill. The third phase will have you do first long intervals and then short intervals. All phases culminate in you being in top form for your race!

Once again, I had to learn all this the hard way so that you don't have to!

When I started running again and training for a half marathon for the first time, my performance on my training runs was incredibly inconsistent. Some runs were great—on others, I totally fell apart. This was particularly true for my long runs. Sometimes, I ended up walking home or taking the bus. It was devastating! If I wasn't fit enough to complete this run, how would I ever be able to move on to even longer runs during my training and finally complete a race?

But then I started analyzing my runs from hell, I realized that they were exactly as inconsistent as my preparation was. Some days I would do my long run at the beginning of the day right after breakfast, on others before lunch, or in the late afternoon. On some days, I had drunk plenty of water; on other days, I had forgotten to rehydrate. Some runs I did right after a meal, while on others, my stomach started grumbling halfway through.

I realized that 80 % of the time, if I failed, it was due to one of four reasons: dehydration; running out of carbs; putting myself under too much pressure; or wearing the wrong clothing. Once I started physically preparing for my runs more consciously, I could concentrate on the mental game (see Mental Game chapter), and everything became much easier. I felt much more confident and was less anxious that I might fail.

So, let's get you started on finding a suitable training plan for you, shall we?

HOW TO CHOOSE A TRAINING PLAN

This chapter is designed to help you find the right training plan whether you are currently not doing any sports at all or whether you have run a couple of half marathons but want to get faster or anything in between. (You will find suggestions for specific training plans towards the end of this chapter.)

There are, of course, other ways of getting ready for a half marathon. You might find that you want to invest in a **personal trainer** or join a **running group** that specializes in getting you ready for a half marathon. Either one can be a good alternative or supplement to manage your training.

In this chapter I am going to talk you through:

- the **different running elements** you might find on your training plan
- more **details on training zones**
- what considerations to make when **picking a training plan**
- the pros and cons of the **different intensity monitoring methods**
- **specific training plan suggestions**
- There are three aspects where one training plan may differ from another: **workout types, method of intensity measurement, and intensity zones**.

WORKOUT TYPES

Training plans usually contain **workout types that have different effects on your body**. A training plan to get you off the couch and start running might contain primarily walking and only a few running elements at first. There will also be different lengths of runs and walks. Once you get into more advanced training plans, they frequently add more elements such as tempo runs and interval training.

Each of these different types of workouts are performed at a specific intensity level to yield a specific result. (See my remarks on periodization above.)

Depending on your starting point and your training goal, the training plan that's best for you might look quite different from somebody else's.

If you are just starting out as a runner, your training plan may include **walking/running, easy runs, long runs, or tempo runs**. If you are a more advanced runner, you might also find **interval training** and other elements on your training plan.

Walking

If you are just getting off the couch, then some of your training in the beginning might be walking to get your body going and also to **strengthen your muscles and joints**. Walking can also be a good cross training or recovery activity after a particularly strenuous workout. Don't skip it!

Running/Walking

As your journey as a new runner progresses, you will start to **combine walking with some running**. In the beginning, a workout might consist of you walking to warm up, followed by one minute of running, followed by two minutes of walking. You will repeat this several times before doing a cooldown walk again.

Run/walking helps build up muscles so that you can start running continuously.

As a runner advances to a stage where they **can run at an easy pace**, workouts will start including the following elements:

Easy Runs

These runs make up the **majority** of your training plan. They are run at an easy pace where you can still **keep up a conversation in full sentences**. These easy miles allow your muscles to learn to use oxygen more efficiently and thereby enable you to run more intense workouts (including the race). An additional benefit is that the easy runs also build **cardiovascular fitness**, which will help you to progress to more advanced types of running elements.

Long Runs

Long runs are usually done **once a week**, frequently on the weekends as most people have more time then. The purpose of the long run is to **increase your endurance**. During these long runs, your muscles adapt to using oxygen more efficiently. Also, your body gets used to **burning fat** more efficiently (instead of just carbohydrates). A further benefit is that your body learns to **deal with muscular fatigue** to be able to run longer distances.

Tempo Runs

A tempo run is **faster than the long and easy runs**. The pace will be a **little slower than your 5k race pace**, which is the fastest you could run 5k. When you run relatively fast, your body produces lactic acid, and this can cause an uncomfortable feeling in your legs. The tempo runs help your body to become more efficient at **clearing the lactic acid from your muscles**, allowing you to **run at a faster pace for longer**.

Striders

Striders are runs where you **start slow and accelerate to nearly top speed** over a short distance. Striders are a great way to warm up for runs with speed work, e.g. intervals or fartlek runs.

Intervals

Intervals are highly structured workouts that follow a **hard effort** of a particular distance and then a set amount of **rest**.

Fartleks/Speed Plays

"Fartlek" is a Swedish term that means "speed play." Fartleks are a rather unstructured, playful way to include speed and faster segments into your training runs. After warmup, you simply mix segments of medium to hard effort with less-strenuous segments of different or similar lengths.

INTENSITY MEASUREMENT

There are three main ways that I recommend to establish your training intensity. The most customary methods are **pace** and **heart rate monitoring**. Heart rate training can be done with a heart rate monitor chest strap which connects to a training watch, with an activity tracker, or with a smartphone. (Some watches measure the heart rate on your wrist so you don't need a chest strap, but this may not be as reliable/accurate. See Equipment chapter.)

If you train by pace, you can measure it with a GPS-enabled smartphone and app, a foot pod, or a GPS-enabled training watch.

The third, more recently developed method to measure running intensity is power. **Power** can be measured in several ways, e.g. by **foot pod, chest strap, or integrated in the running watch**.

Yet another method, **Perceived Exertion**, asks you to listen to your body and judge your intensity yourself. Perceived Exertion is great to accompany other methods as you begin to build a better awareness of your body while you run. It can work for more experienced runners, but I suggest sticking to one of the other methods if you are not a super-seasoned runner yet.

As mentioned at the beginning of the chapter, not all training elements are run at the same intensity level. Therefore, there needs to be a way to establish how much effort you need to put into your running to perform the different elements at the correct intensity level. **Running intensity is established through training zones.** In the following section we are going to go through this topic in more detail.

TRAINING ZONES

Different training plan creators have different ways of establishing training zones. To get the best results, **I suggest you use the method recommended by the training plan you choose**. I will take you through one example in this chapter, so you can get a rough idea of what they could look like.

There are good reasons to use training zones. If you misjudge your effort and run too fast—for example, when you are doing a tempo run or intervals—you might fade away during the workout and not be able to complete it as planned. If you run too slowly, then you will likely not achieve the **desired training effect**. The intensity zones will help you pace yourself correctly to get the biggest benefit out of your workout. If you are just starting with walking or run/walking, then zones will be less important for you at this stage. They will gain significance as you progress.

Types of Training Zones

Martti Karvonen, a Finnish physician, did some of the earliest research work on training intensities. He published his formula in 1957. The Karvonen method uses **Heart Rate Reserve** to calculate the zones, whereas some of the methods developed later are based on different anchor points such as **Threshold Heart Rate**, which is the maximum heart rate that you can sustain over a longer period of time, e.g. around 30 to 60 minutes.

I will now walk you through one of these zone systems so that you can get a rough idea of what the one you will use might look like.

Polar is a company that was established in 1977. They develop heart rate monitors to measure a person's heart rate during sports.

The table below shows you how the **Polar Heart Rate Zones** are established and gives you an idea of one possible method. Most of the other methods you will find in the industry are similar. Some can vary on what they use as an anchor point to calculate the zones—for example **threshold pace instead of maximum heart rate**—or the basis for calculating the actual zones, e.g. heart rate reserve. In case you are curious what max heart rate is, that's the maximum rate at which your heart will beat when you give your max effort. I would not worry about these technical details. **Your training plan should include detailed instructions of how to calculate your zones in the intensity measurement method you are using**, i.e. heart rate, pace, or power.

Zone	% effort of max heart rate	Description & Benefits	What It Feels Like
Very light	50 to 60	This is the recovery zone, often used on days after hard efforts as active recovery.	• can run for a very long time • will easily be able to talk
Light	60 to 70	In this zone, you are improving your endurance. Your body also learns to use fat as a source of fuel.	• still feels relatively easy • be able to run for a significant amount of time • can hold a conversation with a running buddy
Moderate	70 to 80	In the moderate zone you are improving your aerobic fitness. This is also the zone where lactic acid starts to build up. In this zone your body is still able to clean out the lactic acid, and your running will not be affected.	• breathing starts to become a little more rapid
Hard	80 to 90	In zone four, you'll be improving your endurance to run at higher speeds. Your body is also learning to burn carbs and to tolerate higher lactic acid levels in this zone.	• breathing quite rapid • muscles feel fatigued
Very hard	90 to 100	This is the all-out zone! In this zone, you'll be giving all you can give. Your lactic acid buildup will be significant.	• breathing very rapid • muscles may feel sore • feel as if you can't continue to move at all, almost as if you were running in slow motion • will not be able to stand this zone for more than five minutes • beginners will most likely not use this zone

Different Zones for Different Sports

The zones are **not the same for all sports**. According to Polar, for **cycling** the zones are about **five to ten beats lower** than for running, and **for swimming** they are about **another five to ten beats lower** than for cycling.

Calibration of Zones

The one good thing about **heart rate zones** is that they **only change with age**, but not as your fitness progresses. When you're getting fitter, you will just be running faster at the same heart rate.

With pace and power zones, you will need to recalibrate about once a month to still be training at the correct intensity. The reason is that as your speed and endurance increases, you will be running faster in each of the zones, and your pace and power that used to correspond to a certain intensity will no longer feel as intense. This means you will need to recalibrate your zones periodically.

When you recalibrate your zones, you redo the test to find your new zones. You can look back and see how much faster you are running in specific zones compared to the beginning of your journey. This will give you some indication of how much impact your training has had. You will likely see that you are getting faster on each recalibration. These are always fun moments!

CONSIDERATIONS TO MAKE WHEN CHOOSING A TRAINING PLAN

I have included several very specific training plan recommendations at the end of this chapter, but if you would like to find your own training plan, this section will be particularly important for you.

Your Starting Point

Probably the most important consideration to make is where you are starting off. Are you a runner that has just completed a half marathon and wants to get faster, or have you never run before in your life? I would caution you to **be brutally honest with yourself on this question**. Your journey will be more enjoyable and less prone to injury if you start with the right training from the get-go. Starting with a training plan of the wrong level can be very frustrating.

If you have already done some running or even racing recently, then you might want to start the training journey with a **half marathon training plan** straight away. If you have been sedentary for many years, then you might prefer starting with a **Couch to 5k** program and progress from there. If you've never run in your life, you may even want to start with one or several weeks of continuous walking (30 minutes, four days a week, alternating with three rest days a week) before you start running at all.

Like so many other things, I did it the worst conceivable way myself: When I started running again after a 13-year hiatus, I didn't use any training plan at all. I just went out there and tried to get as far as I could to accumulate as many steps as I could for my corporate challenge (see My Life As a Runner chapter). I remember starting off running like crazy and then having to stop totally out of breath all the time.

When I talked about it to my husband one night, he said, "If you have to stop, then you are running too fast." He was so right. I WAS running way faster than my body could handle at that stage.

Over the next couple of runs, I took the pace down several notches. As a former sprinter, that was not easy. And YES, it seemed SUPER SLOW! I felt like I was hardly moving and that people must be pointing and laughing at me. The truth is that most people run too fast. I just reminded myself that I was on a mission and that it did not matter how slow or fast I ran, if only it would help me get fit again.

When I started preparing for my first half marathon, I used the Ten-Week Runner's World First-Timer's Half Marathon Plan. I felt this was a super-good investment because it led me through my training step by step. It gave tips each day, which I really enjoyed. I also felt like it was well constructed, and it did not totally overwhelm me like some of the other ones had done in the past. In addition, it included daily information on different topics such as final race prep or recovery fueling. I learned a lot from these tips, and it felt a bit like constantly having a coach by my side.

So, if you are a novice runner or first-time half marathon runner, do yourself a favor: use a training plan and pick one that's right for your situation. It will take you where you want to be in no time, minimizing your risk for injury.

Starting Mileages and Longest Continuous Run

If you have already been running for some time, then you will already be running a **certain number of miles each week** and possibly doing a long run as well. These are important metrics to consider when picking a training plan. Most training plans state how long you have to be **able to run continuously**.

By the time I transitioned to half marathon training, about a month or two after I had taken up running again, I could run about 30 to 45 minutes without too much trouble. I was not cruising at top speed, but I did not have to stop to catch my breath. I had learned to pace myself, which was the hardest part for me. Now I had to learn to slow down and run at a pace that I could sustain for an hour and then build up to be able to run for two hours.

Many of you will have started from zero and built up your fitness to a point where you can continuously run for a certain amount of time. Congratulations! Time to transition to a half marathon training plan!

Training Time

Besides your starting point, another important consideration to make is **training time**.

For most distances there are **higher- and lower-volume plans**. The volume of training also determines how many hours a week you train. For most half marathon plans, you will be training **3 to 5 times a week including a longer run on the weekend**. This can be a significant time commitment towards the end of the plan as you get closer to the race, so it makes sense to give your partner, family, or friends a heads-up ahead of time. (I found that my family got a bit grumbly each time I hit the one-and-a-half-hour mark on my long runs.) **As a minimum**, you should expect to put **3 to 4 hours a week** aside for running towards the end of the plan.

This might sound like a daunting amount of time at first, but to be honest, when I hear that busy parents with four or five kids and full-time jobs are able to get their training in, then I guess most of us can, too! Sometimes you might have to be a bit creative and do a higher load of cross training instead of running to be more flexible. **Most training plans leave leeway for cross training on a treadmill, bike, or elliptical runner (see Cross Training chapter).**

When my son was about six years old, my husband spent about three months abroad while I was training on a high-volume plan. On some days I was running twice a day. Since I had to bring my son to school and pick him up again in the afternoon, I didn't have enough hours in my day to get all my running done. So, I had to get creative. I completed my first run of the day during lunch time and did my second run on the elliptical runner at home in the evening, right after coming home. This way I did not have to inconvenience my son to come along on the trail or to the gym, and I could still have an eye on him while I was training at home.

METHODS TO MEASURE YOUR INTENSITY

As mentioned earlier in this chapter, you can measure your running intensity and determine your running zones with different measuring devices. **They each have their pros and cons.** You might be set on one specific method because you already have the **equipment**, or you might **first decide on the training plan to use** before you decide on the method.

The choice you make is very personal and entirely up to you. Here are some points to take into consideration: **if you have just started running, you probably don't need to invest in much intensity measurement equipment, right away**. If you have a smartphone, you can record your workouts with an app, but most of the time you will be walking or running at a comfortable pace in a low-intensity zone. The most important indication for running in the beginning is that you can do it at a **conversational pace**, which means you can have a conversation while running without getting out of breath.

If you have already done some running and if you own a **GPS-enabled phone or training watch** that is relatively responsive, then **pace zones** can be ideal. Response time is essential, though. If you come to a complete stop, for instance, you don't want your watch to take 15 seconds to show you at zero miles per minute pace. You want it to react almost immediately. When you do intervals, you change pace rapidly and frequently, usually within 30 seconds to two minutes, and you certainly want your watch to adjust quickly within a 30-second interval, so responsiveness, again, is of importance.

In my experience, **pace zones work quite well if you are training in a relatively flat area**. If you train in more hilly areas, then pace can be difficult to stick to. In those cases, I would usually refer to my heart rate zones.

My personal preference—although more expensive—has been to train with power. You will need a special device for that, such as **a foot pod, a hip pod, or a training watch with a power meter built in**, which can tell you your running power in Watts, rather than in minutes per mile (pace) or heart rate. In other words, it's another way to measure the intensity you are training at. (If you want to look into this method of training with power or you are flirting with the idea to change to this method, the link I provide in the reference section will get you started on the benefits of training with power and how it's done.)

I started doing this in 2018 and absolutely love it now. I find it to be the **most accurate on most terrains**. The only downside is that there are still **many training plans that are not issued in power, and most of the ones that are tend to be more advanced training plans**.

I suggest you make the decision based on the equipment you already own, what is offered by the training plans you like, and what your gut feeling tells you.

In the next sections you will find some more details for each of the different methods to measure intensity.

Heart Rate Monitoring

If you want to use heart rate as your measure of intensity, you will either need a **heart rate monitor chest strap** that you can connect to your training watch, e.g., via Bluetooth, or you will need a watch which has a **built-in heart rate monitor** that measures your heart rate at your wrist.

Another point to check before buying one is if it's **compatible** with the phone or app that you are using.

Heart Rate Monitoring Pros	Heart Rate Monitoring Cons
• a large number of training plans available • only very infrequent zone recalibration necessary	• can vary from day to day depending on temperature, hydration level, sleep, etc. • will likely require additional equipment • heart rate adjusts relatively slowly and can be tricky to gauge your intensity when doing shorter intervals

Pace-Based Intensity Measurement

For pace-based measurement you will need a GPS device or foot pod.

Pace-Based Intensity Measurement Pros	Pace-Based Intensity Measurement Cons
• may not require additional equipment if you are using your phone for tracking your workouts • does not vary depending on your daily form influenced by e.g., temperature, hydration level, sleep, etc.	• requires zone recalibration about once a month • difficult to use in hilly areas

Power-Based Training

Power-based devices are great when you are getting more serious about running. I can **highly recommend them for more experienced runners if you can find a fitting plan**. I don't advise them for novice runners, since there are not many power-based plans for runners that are just starting out. I do propose to do your research if you decide to buy a running power meter. Some training watches and chest straps measure power, but you may need to check their **accuracy**.

Power-Based Training Pros	Power-Based Training Cons
• generally, more accurate for hills; some even consider wind • doesn't depend on your daily form • depending on device it can adjust relatively quickly for short intervals	• least number of training plans available (but it's getting better); still relatively few for novice runners • most likely you will need an additional device, e.g., a foot pod • periodic zone recalibration necessary • not native to some watches, therefore not all features may be available with certain training watches

Personally, I have had training plans that have used all three of the measurement-based methods. On my first training plan, I trained on heart rate. This was not bad, but it did vary quite a lot from day to day how I felt at the same pulse. On some days, I felt like I was hardly moving when my pulse was sky high, and on other days, it felt like I could not get my pulse up to the necessary level no matter how fast I ran. When I did tempo runs or intervals—paces I did not spend a large chunk of time training at—it became difficult to pace because of the delay in heart rate adjustment when my pace changed.

On subsequent training plans, I trained with pace zones, which worked in flat areas, but was an issue when the terrain was hilly—this led me to pick mainly flat training routes—that did not help build power. If I had a longer uphill or downhill piece, I would run by pulse since the pace zones did not correspond to the correct intensity.

Eventually, I transitioned to power—this has fully met my needs in basically every aspect. It adjusts very quickly; it doesn't vary with temperature and hydration level as my pulse did. Overall, the training experience felt a lot smoother and more consistent. My power meter is about four years old, and technology has evolved quite a bit on them, so I could imagine that the current technology is a great pleasure to use.

HOW TO DECIDE ON A TRAINING PLAN

We have arrived at the last step: picking your training plan. There are some choices to make at this stage: paid vs. free; app vs. paper vs. having the whole thing on a platform. I will talk you through some of these last decision points before I recommend a few training plans which might be appropriate for your journey.

A word of caution before we get started, though: even as I recommend getting a training plan to guide you through your training process, it's just as important to develop a good sense for what is going on with your own body, as well. Don't follow your training plan blindly if your body screams, "NO!"

For instance, a grueling high-intensity interval workout might not be such a good idea if you've just returned from a double graveyard shift. If you feel a bit under the weather for whatever reason, swapping the days of your workouts or skipping a workout on a rare occasion might serve you better in the long run than strict execution of your training plan to the letter. (If, however, you find yourself skipping or switching too many units, it's time to find out why. I will explain potential problems with training plans in the chapter on Motivation.)

Paid vs. Free

What do they say? You get what you pay for. There are plenty of free training plans out there, but will they get you to the finish line the same way as a paid one will? Just the way I urge you to invest in good shoes, I highly recommend a paid plan—at least for the more advanced levels of your training. **There are some good, well-established free plans for the start of your journey such as the Couch to 5k plan**, which gives you a perfect start. **For the half marathon training part, though, I propose a paid plan.** A half marathon training plan will likely cost you in the range of about $10 to $40, depending on whether you get it in print or via an app or platform.

There are several reasons why I prefer a paid plan for the later training phases. The first comes back to the one topic that I have been harping on the whole book: **injury**

prevention. If you invest in a paid plan by a reputable coach, they will have designed it in a way that your body gets enough recovery time to be able to handle the increase in load each week.

Secondly, most paid plans are put together by coaches that have trained many athletes. They have put a lot of thought, expertise, and experience into these plans, which will likely yield a **good result**, meaning they will most likely train you better for speed and endurance.

Paper vs. Platforms vs. Apps

Whether you get a training plan in an app, on a platform such as TrainingPeaks™ or Final Surge™, or on paper is your personal choice. There are different pros and cons to each option and some differences in price.

If you get a training plan on paper, you get the satisfaction of checking off your workouts with a pen or pencil. It's usually the **lowest cost** option, but it doesn't offer you easy ways to **compare** your workouts over time.

If you purchase a training plan that is uploaded on a **platform such as TrainingPeaks™ or Final Surge™**, you will likely be able to upload your workouts from many different sources, i.e., watches, trackers, and apps.

At the time of writing, both the TrainingPeaks™ and Final Surge™ basic accounts were free. With a basic plan you were able to get summaries of your workouts as well as daily workout reminders and to upload many different types of training plans. The workouts also synced automatically from your training watch of several brands. Therefore, if you choose to use training plans from different providers in the future, it's quite possible that they will also integrate them on TrainingPeaks™ or Final Surge™, and you can keep all your history in one place. If you are into analyzing things, then the premium plans are for you. There is a fee for this.

Apps have the plus that they often allow you to connect with other users so you can **share your workouts with running buddies or friends**. Or sometimes you can join **leaderboards and challenges** where you can compete against each other for mileage per week or other metrics (see Strava, for instance). It's a fun way of gamification to stay motivated.

SUGGESTED TRAINING PLANS

Whichever plan you decide to start with, there is one very important point to keep in mind. If you feel the plan is stretching you too far from your comfort zone, **reconsider**! The plans should focus on a **gradual progression** from where you are starting. Remember: you want to get to the start line of your race injury-free and feeling fit, not overtrained. Even if you have a training plan that is at the right level, keep in mind that on certain days you may not feel up to scratch to do the assigned workout.

Starting from the Couch

If you are just starting out, the most important thing will be to get you to a point where you can **run continuously before you go on to the half marathon training**. There are a couple of good programs to do this, sometimes with telling names such as "Couch to 5k" (C25k) or "Run Your Butt Off!" Starting to run when you have been sedentary for a long time is demanding for your heart, lungs, muscles, bones, and joints. A good novice plan will likely start with **walking** at first to strengthen your limbs and joints and prevent injury. As you become fitter, you will do workouts where you spend short amounts of time running and then walking again. You will do this until you build up to being able to run for about 30 minutes.

I suggest you run a 5k race once you have completed the C25K program. This way, you will get some experience, and the half marathon won't be your first race, so it won't feel as daunting.

It is very likely that you will still walk parts of the 5k race, and it might take you longer than 30 minutes, but this doesn't matter. It's all about the spirit of participation and getting a race under your belt!

Here is the path I suggest:

Step 1

Choose one of the following plans that will get you moving gradually and gently if you have never run before or have not run in a long time. These plans will get you running for about 30 minutes at once. At this stage you should be ready to run a 5k race, even if you need to take a couple walking breaks.

- *Runner's World* "Run Your Butt Off!"
- OR "Couch to 5k (C25K)" Training Plan

Step 2

As a second step, once you have completed an intro plan to get you running continuously, you are ready to start half marathon training with an introductory half marathon plan. This is also a plan that you can come back to if you are looking for a lower volume or a plan with a lower time commitment.

- 80/20 Running: 2021 Edition Half Marathon Level 0 (or more recent edition, if applicable)

Between steps one and two, you will go from running three times a week to running five times a week, but slightly shorter distances. If you would like to make this transition more gradually, you can repeat the last weeks of your step one plan for a couple more weeks (as many as you feel appropriate) and add 1 to 2 more days of running a week until you feel ready to move on to the half marathon training plan.

*Starting from Completion of "C25K,"
"Run Your Butt Off!" or Weekly Running Duration
of About 90 Minutes*

If you have successfully completed the "Couch to 5k" plan, Runner's World's "Run Your Butt Off!", or another introductory running plan, or if you are running about 90 minutes weekly, then you can go straight on to half marathon training.

If you want to make the transition a bit more gradual, you can increase your weekly duration and running time by **building up to 4 to 5 runs of 25 to 30 minutes a week before going on to the half marathon plan**.

The following training plan is a good transition after the Couch to 5k plan or Run Your Butt Off! plan, as it starts at a relatively low volume and doesn't jump the mileage too quickly.

- 80/20 Running: 2021 Edition Half Marathon Level 0

Starting Mileage Around 14 mi (22 km) per Week, Longest Runs Around 4 to 6 Mi (6.4 to 9.6 km)

If you are already running and your starting mileage is between 12 to 14 miles (19 to 22 km) per week, or you can run at least 4 to 6 miles (6.4 to 9.6 km) at once, then you might consider taking a **more advanced half marathon plan** such as:

- Hal Higdon: Half Marathon Training: Novice 1
- 80/20 Running: 2021 Edition Half Marathon Level 1

The Hal Higdon plan starts with a **4 mi (6.4 km) long run in the first week** and the 80/20 plan with a **50-minute long run**. Depending on how fast you are running, you might find one or the other more suitable.

I used the 80/20 Running Half Marathon Level 1 plan to train for my second half marathon.

If this is your first half marathon, however, and you are not a total running pro yet, I would stick to a novice/

first-timer plan, as these usually provide you with some additional advice and support for your first race.

*Been Running for a Year or More
or Want to Run a Faster Half Marathon*

If you have been running for more than a year and you are interested in a more advanced plan, or perhaps you have already run a half marathon and are looking to become faster, then the following could be plans for you to consider:

- Hal Higdon: Half Marathon Training: Novice 2
- Hal Higdon: Half Marathon Training: Intermediate 1 or 2
- 80/20 Running: 2021 Edition Half Marathon Level 1
- 80/20 Running: 2021 Edition Half Marathon Level 2
- Runner's World: Beginners Half Marathon Plan
- Runner's World: Intermediate Half Marathon Plan

I suggest you read about the **starting requirements** for each plan carefully and decide for yourself which one suits you best. Some of these plans really kick it up a notch and get you running or cross training nearly every day. Also, you want to seriously consider how much time you are willing to spend exercising each week, as some of them take a significant amount of time out of your schedule.

Now that you know all about training plans and why they are important, you have completed one more step in preparing for your half marathon. The last step on training plans is simply making your choice and selecting one! It's a fun process.

In summary:

- A well-structured training plan helps you to train effectively and safely, avoiding injuries and overtraining. It will tell you what type of training to do when, at what intensity, and when to rest and recover.
- There are different methods to measure intensity: heart rate, pace, and power.
- Different training plans may require a higher or lower volume of training; also, they may start relatively easy but build up considerably towards the race.
- You should never increase your mileage by more than 10 to 15 % per week!
- If you notice any onset of an injury or knee, foot, or hip issues, it's best to have it checked medically straight away. Don't wait until it turns into an actual problem. Sometimes the fix can be very simple, such as the prescription of orthotics.

CROSS TRAINING

You might have come across the term "cross training" before and wondered what it meant, why runners do it, and what its relationship is to recovery. **Cross-training is a sport other than running that a runner engages in to supplement their endurance training to either increase their endurance, increase their strength and power, or to recover from strenuous training or a race.** A runner might choose to cross train when they recover from injury or to prevent it, to recover from strenuous efforts, or to strengthen muscle groups in a more efficient way than is possible with running, for instance with **specific strength training**. Some runners simply enjoy mixing in some other sports to have some **variety**.

I, personally, have used cross training very sparingly, simply because I love running best. And for a very long time, I didn't have any injuries to overcome, either. For others, it can be a godsend, either because they love other sports or because they need it to get over an injury. **Running is a high-impact sport; by substituting it with other endurance sports and supplementing it with strength training, the stress on our bodies from running can be minimized.** For athletes who have had injuries in the past or are particularly injury-prone, cross training can become an **essential part of their training strategy**.

Here are some of the main reasons why you may want to consider including cross training in your training routine:

INJURY PREVENTION AND RECOVERY FROM INJURY

Some runners are more injury-prone or might have suffered an **injury** in the past and therefore want to take precautions not to get re-injured. In this case, they may choose to **minimize the high impact of running** by cross training in other activities such as **cycling, aqua jogging, running on an elliptical, or swimming**. By replacing some of the runs with another sport, runners can still **build strength, speed, and endurance, just more gently**, avoiding the high impact of running to help reduce the stress on the body.

A runner might temporarily replace their running with cross training entirely if they have suffered an injury. For example, a runner with a leg injury might temporarily switch to aqua jogging or cycling for some time, if the injury permits, as these are **lower-impact sports**.

I trained with a team from age 9 to 22, and that meant that I was extremely careful not to get injured. Most of my coaches had their antenna out for injuries among us athletes and would send us off the track to get checked out at even the slightest hint of an injury. There's a good reason for that. **Catching injuries at the onset makes it FAR easier to treat them.** So, I never really had a reason to do anything else but running. However, when I got injured for the first time in my running life recently, I was extremely happy to be able to switch sports. I rented a stationary bike, and even though I missed running, I was content that it allowed me to exercise regularly while my tendonitis was healing.

My husband came to cross training in pretty much the opposite fashion; unfortunately, he had to learn it the hard way.

When he was in his 20s, he trained for a marathon. Regrettably, he was too ambitious and increased his weekly mileage from 30 to 60 miles (48 to 96 km)—way too fast. (**You should never increase your mileage more than 10 to 15 % from one week to the next.** See Training.) He got to the start line with pain in his knee, and after seven miles, the race was over for him. He had to hobble to the next streetcar to meet his friend at the finish line, suffering mockery by the onlookers.

The doctor told him that if he still wanted to run in his 50s, he should consider doing some of his endurance exercise in a different sport. Since he is an avid cycler, that wasn't a problem. But as the years went on and I had started running again, he also partook in the fun, and soon the pain in his knee was back… This time the doctor prescribed orthotics, and he was off to the racetrack again.

A few years later, he developed tendonitis under his foot, so he had to switch back to hold off running again. Once his foot had recovered, he was advised to restart running very slowly and carefully, 5 to 10 minutes of running at most. After a few relapses of the foot problem, he decided that he would be stronger and fitter if he did various sports. Although he can do more running now, he has decided to make his fitness routine into a **multi-sport undertaking**, including everything from trampolining, swimming, cycling and unicycling, to strength training and yoga. **He loves it, and it's helped him stay injury-free.**

RECOVERY

Cross training can **speed up recovery** after hard or long workouts or races. Getting off your feet and into the pool or onto a bike can help **circulate more oxygen** into your muscles without the impact of pounding the pavement, which can help runners recover faster.

Sometimes in the summer after my long runs or interval workouts, I love to go for a gentle swim in the pool the next day. In the past, I have also sometimes replaced my long runs with very long pool swims. I don't feel that they are as good of a workout, but every so often on vacation, when a long run was complicated to organize, I opted for a long swim instead.

BUILDING STRENGTH

Runners will also cross train to **build strength**, for example through **strength training**. Strength training allows muscle group isolation, such as the core, which is very important **for running** but can't easily be built up **by running**. (Some people argue that strength training is not cross training but an additional activity that supports your running.)

Strength training is advisable as an injury prevention measure and to build core strength. I would like to do more of it, but I must admit it is not my strong point. It is highly advisable, though! When I was training to PR (i.e., training to reach a new personal record), I have worked strength training into my weekly exercise routine, and I always felt it had a very positive impact on my training, making me a faster and more powerful runner. Some training plans have strength training routines that come with them; others offer them separately.

Strength training routines can include anything from push-ups to planks, squats to sit-ups, pull-ups to lunges, you name it. Some will center around core strength, others around leg strength and power.

TRAVEL, WEATHER, AND OTHER REASONS TO CROSS TRAIN

If I turn to cross training, it's usually due to some sort of travel. For instance, when I used to visit my mom in California, where it was often quite **hot outside**, I would sometimes trade in the trail or road for the pool, especially if I didn't make it to my run in the cooler morning hours.

Other times, when I travel to a new or less safe city, especially in winter, with **few daylight hours**, I prefer cross training **at the hotel gym** to running outside. It just feels **safer** to me.

And there is one last reason for me to NOT go running outside: ice! **Icy weather conditions** are almost the only ones that I fear and try to avoid. In my opinion, it's far too risky to pull a muscle or ligament on slippery ground. So, when it's icy outside, watch Beverly fall in love with her elliptical runner!

SPORTS TO CONSIDER FOR
CROSS-TRAINING

Sport	Pros	Cons
Cycling	• Builds strength • Builds cardio fitness • Low impact	• Needs special equipment • May not be suited in all areas depending on available roads or trails (of course, there's indoor cycling on a stationary bike, too, which makes you independent of weather and terrain, but which some people find a bit tiresome)
Swimming	• Builds cardio fitness • Low impact	• Needs access to a pool or open water
Elliptical Running	• Similar activity to running • Low impact	• Needs access to an elliptical runner • Some people find this activity very monotonous
Aqua Jogging	• Similar to running • Builds strength • Builds cardio fitness • Low impact	• Needs access to a pool
Cross Country Skiing (also called Nordic Skiing)	• Similar activity to running • Builds cardio fitness • Low impact • Great activity in winter when running (or cycling) may be difficult to do	• Needs special equipment • In most areas, it will be possible only in certain seasons

It's worth keeping an open mind when it comes to trying a new sport for cross training purposes. My husband, for instance, never felt like much of a swimmer. But he did need an alternative for when cycling wasn't feasible in winter. Eventually, he took some swimming lessons to feel more agile in the water. Soon, he began to love it and signed up for swim training every weekend. It became a new and essential part of his sports routine.

OTHER SUPPLEMENTAL ACTIVITIES BENEFICIAL FOR RUNNERS

As mentioned before, cross training **activities that are similar to running will be more beneficial to your training** than sports that are very different from running. However, there are certain activities that will benefit your running in other ways, even though they won't help you to build endurance. I would include strength training and yoga in this category.

Sport	Pros	Cons
Strength Training	• Builds strength • Strengthens essential body areas important for running which are not strengthened by running, e.g., core	• May need some professional instruction • May need additional equipment unless doing body weight training
Yoga	• Requires little extra equipment • Stretching of the whole body • Great recovery activity if done at low intensity • Great for stress relief	• May need some professional instruction

HOW TO WORK CROSS TRAINING INTO YOUR TRAINING PLAN

Many good training plans contain suggestions for which days you can do cross training. Sometimes these workouts are marked as **optional**. There are many reasons why one would sometimes prefer cross training, including travel, saving time, being able to train at home, at work, or in a gym, or simply because you love other sports, too, and you like mixing it up a bit. A great way to work in cross training would be to **replace a recovery run**, for example, with a leisurely swim or cycle.

You can also replace a shorter run with a cross training session. Keep in mind, though, that you improve at what you practice. You will have to have the majority of your training be running if you want to improve your running. If you can, stick to cross training activities that are as close to running as possible. Choosing activities most comparable to running will help you improve more than if you participate in activities that are very different from running, such as tennis or golf.

An important point to keep in mind is that the cross training activity that you pick and perform should **match the approximate intensity level** of the prescribed training for the day.

Also, if you decide to cross train, it's worth ensuring that you have the **proper equipment with the right fit and that you are using the correct technique and form for the sport**. As with running, you have to use proper techniques to get the best results and stay injury-free in other sports, too. If you are a novice, that might mean taking a few lessons first or signing up for regular training under professional instruction. As my husband's example shows, getting better at something may not only make it more effective, but also **more enjoyable**.

In summary:

- Whether you choose to cross train to add variety to your training, to prevent or recover from injury, to recover from strenuous runs or a race, or to build strength, speed, and power, you can choose from a plethora of different activities, including swimming, aqua jogging, cycling, or the elliptical.
- It's best to stick to activities as similar to running as possible so that the workouts help you build your cardio fitness, strength, and endurance as a runner. Ideally, most of your training should still be running outdoors, if possible.
- It is worth investing in good equipment and getting advice on the proper use of the equipment and proper form to perform the cross training activities.

MOTIVATION

So, you've decided to run a half marathon and started your training full of enthusiasm… and then some doubts crept in. Was it really such a great idea? What if you have bitten off more than you can chew? Can you trust yourself to keep up your training until the race, come rain or shine? And will you be able to pull it off and go the full distance on race day?

It's totally understandable. Training for a half marathon can take you three to five months or longer if you have never run before. In the meantime, you might get swamped with a new project at home or at work, or you might catch a cold that sets you back in your training, and it might jeopardize your motivation.

In this chapter, I will cover some of the challenges you may face and some strategies that will help you stick to your plan and not get distracted from your half marathon journey.

Before I dive in, let me remind you that **one of the most important ways to stay motivated is to review your WHY daily**. It should be your north star. If you ever feel like throwing in the towel, review your WHY and adjust it if necessary.

COMMON CHALLENGES
FOR HALF MARATHON RUNNERS

According to Greg McMillan, founder and head coach at McMillan Running, the top three reasons why runners fail to achieve their goals are as follows:

1. injury
2. low-quality training
3. life-balance

INJURY

I know I've been harping about this the whole book already, but it can't be said enough: **make sure to stay injury-free at all costs! Running is a great sport, but it's not without risk.** Listen to your body and take some time off if you have any aches or pains. If the issue persists or gets worse, seek medical help. Watch for signs of common potential injuries, like **IT Band Syndrome, runner's knee**, or **shin splints**.

If you ignore niggling pains, they can grow into much more significant and more severe problems, which can set you back longer than if you had dealt with the problem early on. By stopping in time, taking a break, and seeking adequate professional help, if necessary, you will be back to running soon without risking long-term damage.

The same goes for illness: **make sure you fully recover** before starting your training again after a cold or flu or any type of infection. Nothing is more devastating than losing additional training time because you did not recuperate thoroughly, and it's an easy trap to fall into.

During your recovery from an injury, **cross training** can be a perfect solution to still get some exercise while staying off your feet (see Cross Training chapter). Discuss what type of cross training would be best with your doctor or physical therapist.

LOW-QUALITY TRAINING

If you find and follow a good training plan, it will give you a good base for high-quality training. Make sure you execute the workouts **as prescribed**, as this can make a big difference in your training progress as well as helping avoiding injury. If you stick to your plan, it will help you train **correctly and efficiently**.

If you find yourself struggling to follow your training plan, consider changing to a different one or adjusting it to your current situation. An unsuitable plan can be just as bad as a poor one to begin with.

Wrong Training Plan

If you feel your motivation dwindling and you dread taking out your training plan, it may simply be because your training plan isn't working for you (anymore). Over time, I've found that every so often, I can't stand my training plan anymore, sometimes simply because I had used it to train for so many races that I got bored with it.

Choosing the wrong training plan or sticking with it for too long is one of the most common reasons for **poor training results and declining motivation**.

Here are some of the issues which may crop up and some possible solutions:

- cryptic terminology
- no indication of running intensity
- wrong level: too hard or too easy

Cryptic Terminology

An interesting phenomenon that is **more common than you would think**: some training plans are so complicated that you simply don't understand what you are supposed to do that day. My first strategy is to avoid these types of plans because if I need a degree in cryptography to decipher them, they're not for me! Most training plans offer a **preview**, so you know ahead or time what to expect.

If you like a specific plan even though it's a bit difficult to understand, study the plan **commentary** and find explanations online. Just expect to spend a bit of time and effort on it.

No Indication of Running Intensity

One of the first training plans I used offered no clear indications of running intensity either by heart rate or pace or any other method. It simply said, "tempo run." To me, that sounded like a quick run, so I ran as fast as

I could on these runs. Having crawled back to the office after my lunch run and having quit several of those runs in the past weeks, I decided to find out how fast I should be running. When I went online and did some research, my suspicion was validated. I was running **WAY too fast**. No wonder I was not able to complete the runs!

Before you start with a training plan, you should check the intensity calculation from your training plan editor. If you don't understand the calculation, you will probably find more information online or by writing to the training plan author. **Once you train at the right intensity, your fitness level will likely improve**, and your recovery periods should become shorter.

Wrong Level

Finding the right plan for your current fitness level and ambition can be tricky. As a word of warning: the first two to three weeks of many training plans are at a pretty leisurely pace and low volume, but they can pick up considerably over time. So, make sure you check further along in the plan to see how many hours and miles you will be running.

It is easy to be full of excitement and overambitious when you are getting started. Remember, the key is to **ramp up slowly**, and a good training plan will help you do exactly that. If you are a novice runner, it's a good idea to stick to a novice plan even if it doesn't seem that challenging at first. And again: **don't increase your mileage more than 10 to 15 % per week!**

When you pick your second plan, you'll be a bit wiser, and you can decide on what other options could be better suited to your pursuit. If you find your training plan is too hard, ensure that you are training at the right intensity. Don't wait too long to adjust your plan. The longer you wait, the more likely you are to injure yourself or suffer fatigue to a point where you will have to take a more extended rest period. If you decide to switch to a lower volume but generally like your plan, the best option could be to stay with the same training plan author and pick their easier plan. Some plans come with a "level guarantee" and will allow you to up or downgrade your plan for free.

LIFE-BALANCE

If there are too many things tugging at your time, e.g., work, family, hobbies, social life, and everything in between, it's easy to become overwhelmed. There are several strategies to avoid getting derailed. In most cases, it helps to **set priorities and stick to them**. This can be difficult at times—there are so many shiny objects out there! But if we focus on fewer priorities, we have a better chance of achieving our goals.

Personally, I noticed that when I reduced my activities down to a manageable number it felt a lot better because I was able to make better progress on all of them. At one point I had been taking piano lessons, writing this book, and practicing public speaking at Toastmasters International, all while spending significant time with our young family and working full-time. I realized I could not "do it all," so I dropped the piano lessons and reduced my efforts in public speaking for a while to focus on my other activities. This is when progress started to happen!

Stressful Phases at Work, at Home, in College

Things can get stressful at times. It helps to be mentally prepared to mitigate difficult circumstances.

The key to getting your workouts done during busy phases is to do them **first thing in the morning**, even if this means waking up earlier. (And being a night owl myself, I'm not stating this lightly!) Chances are that if you hope to run over lunch or after work, something unforeseen will torpedo your plans, or you might feel guilty taking a break during such a stressful phase while everyone else is working hard.

Make sure you are not cutting back on sleep, though! If you are getting up earlier, you should go to bed earlier, too.

Generally, the more stressful life gets, the more you should pay attention to your health habits: eat well, drink enough water, avoid (too much) alcohol, get plenty of sleep, and go outside as much as you can. In fact, exercising can help you cope with stress! Prioritizing sleep and exercise may improve your resiliency when tackling phases of intensive work.

Travel

Another common reason why we may find it hard to work out is travel. As you might have guessed: the solution starts with a plan. **If you have a plan of where, when, and how long to run, that will make it highly implementable.**

Here are some tricks that can help:

- find a running route or gym before you arrive. Alternatively, pick a hotel with running opportunities and/or a gym that fulfills your needs
- find out the time of sunrise and sunset at your destination
- plan your schedule so that you can exercise in the morning
- find out the weather at your destination
- decide on what running clothes to bring
- make a contingency plan, such as cross training, re-planning the workout days of the week, or planning in a recovery week

Find a Running Route or Gym

The easiest way to find a running route is to call the hotel where you will be staying. Many hotels will have running routes that staff can recommend. Ask them to send you a copy of their suggestions so you can **plan your routes and print them out** before you leave home. If you're using your phone or watch to navigate, don't forget to **charge it in time**! In addition, I would always recommend taking a print-out map, as well. You don't want to get stranded in a new place when your phone decides to go nuts and run out of battery quicker than you thought!

Going on a run at your destination can be a great way of getting to know a new place and can be particularly enjoyable if the area is historic or scenic. Some places might even have specific "running sightseeing" options available!

Be careful when asking others about running routes. **Most non-runners will propose very short routes.** What they consider a decent 30-minute run might take you less than ten minutes. Use the suggestions as a starting point for building your route and/or look online for running routes in the area.

Another option is to use sites such as *Great Runs* or apps such as *Strava* or *MapMyRun* to find running routes worldwide. There are, of course, no guarantees with any of these routes. You will have to use common sense and ensure you stay safe. If you're running with a map or device that you have to look at to find your way, **make sure you stop while reviewing the route**. Running and reading maps at the same time is dangerous and can lead to nasty accidents.

Some training watch makers also allow runners to share routes, and this means that you can see if you can find a suitable route in the area. If you are traveling to another office of your company, you can ask your local coworkers, and you might even find a running buddy that way!

If you plan on using the **gym**, you will want to inquire in advance about the opening hours and the equipment. It's worth checking the website for pictures of the gym so you can get an idea. If you like swimming or aqua jogging, you might want to choose a hotel with a **pool**.

Last but not least: whether you run outdoors or in the gym, **always make sure that you are safe**!

Sunrise and Sunset

If you like running during daylight hours, you will need to check on **sunrise or sunset** if you plan to exercise in the morning or evening. I hadn't done all my prework on one trip and found out that at the time I wanted to go running, it was still pitch-black outside! Even if you are in the same time zone on your travel, sunrise and sunset can be at a very different time if you are traveling a significant distance north or south.

Weather at Destination

Make yourself knowledgeable about the weather and climate conditions at your destination. Keep in mind that the weather might deviate from its norm for that time of year and that the mornings and evenings might be significantly colder or warmer than the average temperature. I find running in gear that is too warm for the weather often puts the completion of my workout at risk. If the weather is colder or wetter than you expected, that might make for an equally unpleasant run.

Schedule Your Workouts for the Morning

Frequently on business trips, groups make spontaneous decisions about what to do at the end of the day. Doing your workout in the morning gives you the **flexibility to be spontaneous and social in the evening**.

If you eat before you exercise, you will want to find out what time **breakfast** starts in the morning. If it doesn't fit your schedule, hotel kitchens are often willing to give you fruit or some bread that you can take to your room for the following morning. The alternative is to bring food along—if it's okay to take it on the plane. This way, you know what you get. **Don't forget your water bottles and electrolytes** if you are going on a long run!

Decide What Gear to Bring

If you are going on a short trip, this might be easier since you generally have less luggage. Since the weather is not fully predictable, you have the best chance to hit the sweet spot if you are bringing a couple of different running outfits.

Contingency Plan

Having a backup plan, particularly on a more extended trip, will help you get your workout done. I find it good practice to be equipped with at least one alternative in case there's an issue with my original plan, such as a sudden change in weather, a change of schedule, or a less suitable outdoor running route than I expected.

Here are some possible options that you can combine when you travel (see Cross Training chapter):

- outdoor running
- gym (treadmill, cycling, elliptical runner, stepper, rowing machine)
- swimming or aqua jogging

- cycling (with a rented bike)
- brisk walking

In addition to these rather "technical" potential pitfalls, often runners stop training because they simply lose steam. In my experience, it's common to go through a phase where you question your sanity when you decide to run a half-marathon! If that happens, I find it helpful to review my WHY. After all, there's an overarching goal you want to achieve, right? Here are some **further ideas to jumpstart your motivation**:

Streaking

No, it doesn't mean running around the city naked. It means running at least a short distance **every day, e.g., a mile a day**. So, you could add a short run to your rest/ cross training days just so you will be running every day, including your rest days. This little trick can help you psychologically because you are "**not breaking the chain**." By keeping each run short, it's easier to slot it in and feel good about it every day. Some runners find that very inspiring. Do keep in mind that your body does need rest; therefore, some of these runs should be very short and easy to ensure your body recovers well. If streaking sounds motivating to you, you can even register with Streak Runners International, Inc.

Joining a Running Club

An additional source of motivation can be to run with a local running club at least once a week. Finding people with similar goals and on a similar training level gives you a chance to connect with others who share your hobby—which is good, because, oddly, many non-runners don't appreciate us talking about running all the time!

Finding a Running Buddy

Running with a friend or colleague can be great fun too—if you can make schedules meet and are both committed. Make sure both of you show up at the agreed date and time, though. If either of you has an unpredictable schedule, it could become a burden for the relationship because it's not much fun to be stood up too many times. But if you can make it work, having a running buddy can help you form a habit and also make it a bit more social.

Online Communities

I see many people sharing their running stories online and connecting with other runners, such as in Facebook communities or on Strava. Some runners find these communities incredibly motivating. It can be great fun to post your achievements, stay connected, and cheer each other on. If you don't know that many other runners yet, this can be a way to find motivation and support online.

Just be mindful of what you share online in terms of your running routes, etc., for safety reasons.

Magazines

You might also find some motivation in subscribing to running or endurance exercising magazines such as *Runner's World* for general running articles or *Trail Runner* if you like trail running. They offer plenty of motivating stories and valuable articles to read each month.

Starting Your Own Blog or Facebook Page

Another option is to share your story with the world. Recounting your journey and finding likeminded, kindred spirits can help you stay motivated, especially if running is part of an overarching, life-changing transformation process for you. Perhaps your goal is to lose a significant amount of weight, or you are on the road to recovery after a serious illness or accident. Lots of people have found motivation in sharing their stories and inspiring others with a blog or Facebook Page.

Music, Audiobooks, and Podcasts

One of my favorite motivators is music, particularly for long runs. For music, you might consider running playlists on Apple Music or Spotify. Other options are audiobooks or podcasts. Amazon Audible, for instance, offers a large selection of audiobooks. And there are plenty of running podcasts that can keep you motivated. Just Google and pick your favorite! Any of these can help keeping your brain from "going numb" on long runs.

Movies

Particularly before a race, I love to watch a good running or sports movie. They can really get you hyped up! One of my favorites is *Chariots of Fire*. Rocky is a series of movies our coaches used to show us.

In summary:

- Keeping your motivation up is an important part of your training.
- Common reasons to lose steam include **injury, low-quality training, a poor life-balance, and choosing the wrong training plan**. You can mitigate these problems with attentive planning (including contingency plans).
- Consider adding more fun and a social factor to your running by finding a running club, **running buddies, or supportive online communities**.
- It's also rewarding to read **books and magazines, watch movies, or listen to podcasts** about running.
- Even certain training methods, such as streaking, can rekindle your motivation and keep you going.
- **If you ever feel like giving up, review these strategies and remember your WHY!**

FUELING AND REFUELING

There are many good reasons for eating well. Your body is the only place where you spend your whole life, and therefore it's a good idea to take good care of it. And if you are a runner, you should pay special attention to fueling and refueling your body optimally. Why? First, good fueling will help you reach your **top performance level**. Second, you want to avoid **low energy and psychological stress** during a long run or race. And proper fueling can help **prevent injuries**.

Unfortunately, I learned this the hard way: When I started running again, I was not very conscious about my nutrition. As a result, I had many highly unpleasant training runs which undermined my confidence at the beginning. It was only when I decided that I also wanted to lose some weight that I started researching what it meant to eat healthy. I've never looked back.

Obviously, your **fueling strategy** will be just as unique as your training, based on your physique (body size, shape, and composition), your sex, your training goals, your training level, your food preferences, and the practical circumstances of your daily life.

There is one quote about food I wanted to share. I am a firm believer in Michael Pollan's philosophy: "**Eat food. Not too much. Mostly plants.**" By "eat food," Michael

Pollan means unprocessed food or food without plenty of unpronounceable components in it. Having said that, I try to stick to this "real food" rule most of the time but do allow myself to deviate when it comes to sport gels and carb loaders and sometimes protein drinks or bars out of convenience.

In this chapter you will learn the important components of fueling and refueling for half marathon runners. I will discuss the three **macronutrients, (i.e., carbohydrates, proteins, and fats)**. You will find information in this chapter organized by daily needs, followed by **during** and **post-run** phases.

Before we get started on fueling, I just want to make you aware of the fact that while I am a certified nutrition coach, I don't know your personal medical history. What you will find in this chapter is general guidance that works for most healthy adults. If you have any specific questions or feel that the guidance set forth in this chapter will not be appropriate for your specific needs, you should definitely consult a doctor or registered dietitian nutritionist (RDN) to discuss your specific situation. Keep in mind that every person is different and that the general guidelines may not work for you.

A NOTE ON CALORIES AND CALORIE COUNTING

In the following section, you will find information about the macronutrients you will need each day as well as your daily caloric needs. If you are trying to troubleshoot your diet, then counting calories and types of calories just for one week can be very helpful to understand your baseline. Knowing where the trouble lies will allow you to adjust your diet accordingly. You might decide to count your calories for an additional week while you adjust your diet.

A word of caution, though: If you have a history of eating disorders or calorie-counting has been counter-productive or harmful for you in the past, then counting calories may not be for you. Please be honest with yourself! If you feel that counting calories would lead you down an unhealthy path, then don't do it. If you start and it poses any issue to you, I suggest you stop.

MACRONUTRIENTS

There are **three major types of nutrients** that each have their purpose in a sports diet: **carbohydrates, proteins, and fats**. (Since we need them in relatively large quantities, they are often called macronutrients, as opposed to micro-nutrients such as vitamins and minerals.)

Carbohydrates are particularly important for **fueling your muscles as well as your brain and central nervous system**. Studies have also shown that runners taking in higher amounts of carbs **endure longer and at a faster pace**. Carbohydrates play a special role in fueling your long runs and your races, which is why I have devoted a whole chapter on what's called "carb loading" before the race (see Carb Loading chapter).

Proteins play a key role in **repairing your muscles** after working out. You will need more protein after long runs.

Fat has become the center of a hot debate in sports nutrition lately, spurred by the rise of certain low-carb/high-fat diets such as the popular ketogenic or paleo diets. So, **should you aim to fuel a workout from carbohydrate stores or fat stores**? Based on the research of very well-respected scientists and nutritionists, high availability of **carbohydrates plays a critical role in an athlete's diet**. According to the joint position of the Academy of Nutrition and Dietetics, Dietitians of Canada, and the American College of Sports Medicine, although some benefits might be drawn from a low carb/high fat diet in order to lose body weight or decrease body fat, **your capacity for high-quality and high-intensity workouts is reduced**.

The guidelines I will present to you are based on this research. They are **guidelines for sports nutrition**. If you have specific dietary needs or wishes, such as allergies and intolerances or a vegan or vegetarian diet, you should speak to a registered dietitian nutritionist.

Macronutrients—Your Daily Needs

To understand your macronutrient needs, you need to understand how to calculate your daily caloric intake.

Many of the metrics given in the nutritional world are in grams and grams per kilogram. The easiest thing to do is to convert your weight to kilograms. For this, you can **divide your weight in pounds (lbs) by 2.20 to get your weight in kilograms (kg)**.

Variation by Person and Over Time

As our bodies are different, not everyone needs the same amount of each macronutrient. Keep in mind that as you run you may lose weight and therefore need to **adjust** your daily needs. One piece of advice: be patient! In my experience, a change in my exercise routine or diet usually isn't reflected immediately but only after a couple days to weeks. Additionally, you might actually find that your weight doesn't change much, as you are gaining muscle and losing fat. What you might see instead is that your waist is getting smaller and your clothes are getting looser.

Daily Caloric Need

Before we go through the need for each macronutrient, we are going to find out how many calories you need each day. This will be important to gain the full picture before we get started.

The basic number of calories you need each day is based on your **Resting Energy Expenditure (REE)**. You then add any estimated energy expenditure for your activity level. These activities include everything you do that's not resting (from exercising to walking to climbing stairs to any other physical activity).

A well-established method of calculating the daily caloric need is with the Mifflin-St Jeor Equation: you calculate your REE and then you multiply the result by an activity factor. The Mifflin-St. Jeor Equation was developed in 1990 by Mark Mifflin and Sachiko St. Jeor with the goal of developing an equation to mathematically derive the REE.

Once you know your REE, you apply the Katch-McArdle multiplier that corresponds to your activity level to scale the REE to your daily energy need.

Below you'll find the Mifflin-St. Jeor Equation for women and men:

Women

REE = 9.99 x weight (in kg) + 6.25 x height (in cm) – 4.92 x age (in years) – 161

Men

REE = 9.99 x weight (in kg) + 6.25 x height (in cm) – 4.92 x age (in years) + 5

You'll notice that the equation uses weight in kilograms (kg) and height in centimeters (cm), as opposed to pounds (lbs) and inches (in). Age is in years.

In the following table you'll find the Katch-McArdle multipliers to use for the appropriate activity level.

Activity Level	Description	Multiplier
Sedentary	Office job with little activity	1.2
Lightly Active	Some exercise on 1 - 3 days per week	1.375
Moderately Active	Exercise 3 - 5 days per week	1.55
Very Active	Strenuous exercise 6 - 7 times per week	1.725
Extremely Active	Vigorous daily exercise or strenuous job or training	1.9

Let's take an example: Jane, a 40-year-old woman who weighs 143 pounds, is 5'7" (67 in) tall and runs 4 to 5 times a week for 30 to 60 minutes.

Jane's weight in kg = 143 lbs / 2.2 = 65 kg
Jane's height in cm = 67 in x 2.54 = 170 cm

(The weight and height have been rounded to the nearest kg and cm respectively for ease of use.)

Using the Mifflin-St. Jeor Equation for women, we can calculate Jane's REE to be as follows:

REE = 9.99 x weight (in kg) + 6.25 x height (in cm)
     – 4.92 x age (in years) – 161
   = (9.99 x 65) + (6.25 x 170) – (4.92 x 40) –161
   = 1354 Calories / day

Based on the Mifflin-St. Jeor algorithm, we find that Jane's REE per day is 1354 Cals.

Based on Jane's 4 to 5 runs per week, her activity level would be classified as moderately active. Therefore, her REE would be multiplied by 1.55 to get her daily energy expenditure in calories.

Jane's estimated daily energy expenditure:
1354 x 1.55 = 2099 Cals / day

(From here on, we'll use the approximate number of 2100 Cals / day.)

Protein

Protein is important for metabolic adaptation and muscle repair. Proteins also contain essential amino acids, i.e., amino acids that our body cannot build on its own but needs to absorb from food. Certain essential amino acids are also vital for proper brain function.

Some runners decide to use supplements to cover their protein intake, while others get their protein purely from what they eat. Even for elite athletes, protein supplements aren't necessary but a mere convenience. On the downside, they often don't contain any of the micronutrients and fiber that you get from natural protein sources. If you want to take a protein supplement, I recommend you choose a type with high biological value, e.g., whey protein.

Your daily protein need will likely lie between 1.2 to 2.0 grams per kilogram of body weight. Many recreational endurance runners would fall into the general population category and therefore need to consume protein in the range of 1.2. to 1.6 g/kg body weight. Athletes that are trying to grow their muscle mass would fall into the higher ranges.

Protein has four calories for every gram.

If we take Jane as an example again, and we take a value of 1.6 g/kg body weight, then we get to the following recommended daily protein consumption for her:

Jane's weight in kg (as calculated above): 65 kg
Jane's daily protein need: 1.6 g/kg x 65 kg = 104 g
Daily protein need in Cals: 104 g x 4 Cals/g = 416 Cals

Therefore, Jane needs to consume 104 grams (416 Cals) of protein per day.

By studying the nutrition labels on your food to track your food intake, you can calculate how many

nutrients you get from your foods. Good sources for nutrient-rich protein are as follows:

- lean meat
- poultry
- fish
- soybeans and soy products (e.g., tofu)
- eggs
- low-fat dairy products such as cottage cheese and yogurt
- cheese
- seeds and nuts
- Greek (or strained) yogurt
- legumes such as beans, peanuts, peas, chickpeas, lentils

Fat

In recent years, fats have suffered—undeservedly in part, as it turns out—a bad reputation over decades. We now know that **some fats are much healthier than others** and that high-quality fat is in fact **indispensable** for a healthy diet.

We need fats for **fuel** in the absence of or in addition to carbohydrates, especially for long runs. And they are necessary to absorb some very important micronutrients such as **vitamins A, D, E, and K**.

Avoid the "bad," unhealthy fats wherever possible, especially the kind of **trans fats (also called trans fatty acids)** that are used in margarine, highly processed snacks, and baked goods, as well as when frying or deep-frying fast food. (Smaller amounts of natural trans fats are also found in meat and dairy.) **Trans fats are associated with** coronary artery disease and raising triglyceride levels as well as LDL cholesterol (aka the "bad" cholesterol).

Generally speaking, you should therefore prefer **unsaturated fats (monounsaturated and polyunsaturated)** because they are better for your heart and your cholesterol than saturated fats and can lower the risk of heart disease and stroke.

Fat should make up 20 to 35 % of your daily caloric intake (according to the Institute of Medicine).

Each gram of fat has nine calories.

If we take our favorite runner Jane as an example one more time, we get the following daily need for fat:

Jane's daily caloric needs (previously calculated):2100 Cals

Jane's daily calories from fat: 2100 x 30 % = 700 Cals

Jane's daily energy from fat in grams: 700 / 9 = 78 g

So Jane needs to consume 78 grams (700 Cals) of fat per day.

Good sources for healthy, unsaturated fats are as follows:

- nuts and seeds
- fatty fish such as wild salmon; flaxseeds and flaxseed oil, which are all rich in Omega-3 acids
- avocados
- olives, olive oil, nut oils

Carbohydrates

Carbohydrates have gotten a bad reputation over the years for different reasons. One theory, that carbohydrates make you gain weight, has certainly added to this bad reputation.

To clarify this point, we need to know that there are different types of carbohydrates: simple and complex carbohydrates.

Simple carbohydrates are digested very quickly and are often found in fast food. Fast food, in turn, often contains very few beneficial nutrients such as vitamins and minerals to accompany the simple carbs. Additionally, the trouble with simple carbohydrates is that they can cause our bodies to run out of energy quickly and to get hungry again soon, meaning we eat more calories than we would if we ate the more satiating complex carbohydrates.

Complex carbohydrates keep us feeling full for longer and reduce the risk of calorie overconsumption because of the longer time they take to digest.

Below, you will find an indication of how many carbohydrates you will need during the day depending on how much you are training.

Each gram of carbohydrates has four calories.

Intensity Level	Amount in grams (g) per kilogram (kg) of runner's body weight
Low intensity	3 to 5 g
Moderate intensity level, about one hour per day	5 to 7 g
Moderate to high intensity, about 1 to 3 hours per day	6 to 10 g

Adapted from 2016 Academy of Nutrition and Dietetics & Dietitians of Canada and the American College of Sports Medicine Joint Position Statement: Nutrition and Athletic Performance

Here's the example calculation for Jane's daily carbohydrate need. Remember we calculated that she was 65 kg.

Intensity Level	Carbs in grams (g) per kilogram (kg) of body weight	Daily need in grams (g) per day
Low intensity	3 to 5 g	3 g x 65 kg to 5 g x 65 kg = 195 to 325 g
Moderate intensity level, about one hour per day	5 to 7 g	5 g x 65 kg to 7 g x 65 kg = 325 to 455 g
Moderate to high intensity, about 1 to 3 hours per day	6 to 10 g	6 g x 65 kg to 10 g x 65 kg = 390 to 650 g

Example calculation based on guidance from the 2016 Academy of Nutrition and Dietetics & Dietitians of Canada and the American College of Sports Medicine Joint Position Statement: Nutrition and Athletic Performance

So, Jane would need approximately 195 to 325 g of carbohydrates per day with her activity level. If we multiply that by four calories per gram for carbohydrates, we get a range of 780 to 1300 Cals.

Jane's more precise carb allocation would be calculated with the following formula:

Daily Carb Needs total daily calories – daily calories from protein – daily calories from fats

Pulling all the values together from what we have calculated, Jane's case would look as follows:

2100 Cals daily need – 416 protein Cals – 700 fat Cals
= 984 Cals of carbs

The 984 Cals of Carbs falls in the range of what we calculated for her daily carb needs.
Good sources for nutrient-rich, complex carbohydrates:

• fruit
• sweet potatoes, purple potatoes
• corn
• whole grain bread and pasta
• black and brown rice, quinoa, farro
• oats
• beans, lentils (also a good source of protein)

Macronutrient Timing

In preparation for a half marathon, one important factor to take into consideration with your fueling and refueling strategy is the **timing of your nutrition**. For example, before you go on your weekly **long run**, you would want to make sure you are well **hydrated**, and you also have to make sure you have enough **glycogen (stored carbohydrates)** in your muscles. Being diligent about fueling, starting about four hours before your run, can help you ace your training runs.

After your runs, you will want to make sure that you replenish your glycogen stores and also consume some **protein** to allow for effective muscle repair and recovery.

Once you are in the **final preparatory stages** for your race, you will want to ensure that your **glycogen stores** are at absolute full capacity, so your muscles can draw from them for the longest time possible (see Carb Loading chapter). **During your race**, you will want to make sure that you don't run out of glycogen, so you will want to **refuel** during your long runs and the race as well.

Knowing how to time your nutrition will be very important to get the best out of your training efforts and also your race. In the following sections you will find out how much of each of the macronutrients you will need at what stage.

Before, During, and After the Race

Carb Loading

To ace your race, you want to fuel up on carbohydrates. This is what we call **carb loading**. You will want to **test your carb loading strategy** in the last two to three long runs before your race (see Carb Loading chapter).

During the Race

As your runs start to get longer towards the end of training, you will want to take some fuel along.

See the chart below for **carbohydrate needs** for different lengths of runs.

Duration of Run	Amount of Carbs to Consume
Under 45 minutes	None
45 to 75 minutes	Small amounts, e.g., 4 - 6 oz of sports drink
1 to 2.5 hours	30 to 60 grams per hour

Source: 2016 Academy of Nutrition and Dietetics & Dietitians of Canada Joint Position Statement: Nutrition and Athletic Performance

To satisfy your carbohydrate needs during runs, you can use either **sports drinks** that you can carry with you on a belt, or you can use **energy bars** designed for running. Make sure that the products are appropriate for running. Also ensure that you use the **correct dosing** on the sports drinks in case you have to stir them up from powder. Otherwise, they could upset your stomach.

Some people with sensitive stomachs may not react well to certain carbs and sports drinks. Therefore, it is good to test them ahead of an important training run or race.

After the Race

After a run, your muscles will need some time and fuel to repair. According to a 2016 joint position statement on "Nutrition and Athletic Performance" by the American College of Sports Medicine, **muscle repair can be supported by the intake of 0.25 to 0.30 g/kg of body weight** of high-quality protein within two hours after the run.

OTHER DIETARY NEEDS

If you are a **vegetarian or vegan**, you will likely have to adjust your diet for the additional demand on your body, e.g., making sure you get enough iron and protein.

In any case, listen to your body. You may notice that some of the guidelines don't work well for you, just as your daily calorie intake depends on your metabolic rate, genetics, medication, etc. Try something slightly different and tweak until your fueling strategy fits you, personally!

Last but not least: I highly recommend eating "real food," which means natural, fresh fruit and veggies instead of processed foods; not too much meat; whole grains instead of refined grains (except for the carb loading phases); fresh dairy; and as little refined sugar as possible. And, obviously, leave out anything you are allergic to.

FUELING AND REFUELING—IN A NUTSHELL

I've thrown a lot of information at you, I know. If you are struggling with significant weight, health, or nutritional issues, it is a good idea to talk to a registered dietician nutritionist about your diet.

If you are healthy with a healthy weight and feel no inclination to track your fueling and hydration in great detail, I suggest you simply follow common sense, listen to your body, and remember the main takeaways from this chapter.

In summary:

- Try to eat a **balanced diet** with lots of vegetables and fresh fruit, high-quality meat and dairy, whole grains, nuts, and seeds (**except for the carb loading phase, where you want to take in little fiber** - see Carb Loading chapter).
- **Test all fueling strategies** as well as foods and fueling products diligently before your race. If **carb loading** is for you, start **at least 48 hours in advance** of a half marathon. (see Carb Loading chapter)
- Feel free to revisit this chapter any time you want to recalculate your REE, your daily caloric needs, and your daily intake of the three macronutrients, or if you need to be reminded of good sources for these nutrients.

HYDRATION

At the time of writing, it seems as if many athletes are still mainly concerned about **dehydration**, but less aware of the danger of **overhydrating**. You, too, have probably been told to drink more for most of your life, right? Many runners are encouraged to drink copious amounts of water, and much of the information available doesn't often caution about **overdrinking**.

When you engage in strenuous exercise over a longish period of time, you obviously shed a lot of sweat, which means you lose water and sodium. If you then overload heavily on water, what little sodium is left in your body gets extremely diluted, which means your body can go into a state of **overhydration or hyponatremia (sodium levels in the body that are too low**, as opposed to *hyper*natremia, sodium levels that are too high.) This is sometimes called "**water intoxication**." Severe hyponatremia can cause your brain to swell which, in the worst case, can trigger seizures, a coma, and even death.

Experts on hyponatremia have confirmed that there are still "**misconceptions regarding hydration needs during exercise**," even though the death of two lay marathon runners in 2002 raised public awareness of the problem. Cynthia Lucero (28) collapsed at the 2002 Boston Marathon, her second marathon. Hilary Bellamy (35). She died two days after she overhydrated while racing in the Marine Corps Marathon in Washington D.C..

THE DANGERS OF HYPONATREMIA

Usually, when the sodium levels in our body rise (e.g., because it's hot and we're sweating a lot), we become **thirsty**. If we then drink some water, our sodium levels go back to normal. If we don't, our body holds back as much fluid as possible, which results in more **concentrated urine**.

The danger of **overhydrating** is that the sodium in your body gets so diluted that your electrolyte metabolism goes out of control. Crass overhydration can result in **exercise-associated hyponatremia (EAH)**, a potentially life-threatening condition. For the geeks among you: most labs define the diagnostic threshold for hyponatremia as blood [Na+] below 135 mmol/l and severe hyponatremia as below 120 mmol/l.

According to a 2017 Frontiers in Medicine paper by Tamara Hew-Butler et.al., severe EAH has been reported mostly in endurance athletes **since the 1980s**. The troubling news is that incidences of EAH seem to be on the rise, and it has started to occur in different fields such as the police and the military, and even in low-intensity forms of exercise such as hiking and yoga.

Now that the phenomenon is better known, some race organizers have started putting scales along the racetrack for athletes to weigh themselves at very long races. If you are hydrating well, you should lose a small amount or stay at the same weight. Should you be gaining weight on a long-distance run, it might indicate that you are overhydrating.

To be clear, runners who ended up with severe or fatal EAH had drunk "copious amounts" of water or isotonic beverages, in some cases even in excess of five gallons (20 liters)! You were probably not going to do that anyway. However, **drinking "as much as you can"** used to be a common recommendation for runners for decades, and even official sports organizations have had to adapt their guidelines in recent years, based on the research on EAH.

Note also that **runners** with longer race times may be at a higher risk to overhydrate if they drink too much at every fueling station or within any given amount of time, simply because the race **takes them that much longer**. For the same reason, some experts believe the chances of overhydrating are **lower on a half marathon distance** than on a marathon or ultra-marathon distance.

DRINKING-TO-THIRST VERSUS HYDRATION PLANNING

So, it's your job as a half marathon runner to find a **healthy balance**: not hydrating too little (and risking **lower endurance and cramps due to dehydration**) and not hydrating too much, either (risking overhydration and hyponatremia).

Over the last couple of years, a debate has been raging over the best way to find this balance. There's the "drink-to-thirst" (DTT) camp, which basically argues to trust your own body to know when you need to drink because you start feeling thirsty. The downside of this approach: does "drink-to-thirst" mean you have to drink only when you feel thirsty, or does it mean you should drink to prevent getting thirsty? Also, what if your feeling of thirst is misleading and you do in fact need more or less water than you think? Or if your sweat loss rate is above average? Or if it is much hotter than you are used to? I am looking forward to more research being done in this field.

The other camp in the debate argues for a set drinking schedule because it helps you to reach optimal results exactly because you can plan ahead.

I think I probably fall somewhere in between both camps: my personal strategy is to definitely drink water when I am thirsty, to drink a bit of water several times a day, and to drink water during runs that are over an hour.

Keep in mind, too, that hydration needs are highly dependent on you as an individual, and on your running situation. Runners who sweat profusely will need more water than others.

How much I drink depends on several other factors, too. For instance I find that my habits vary whether I am at work, running errands, or on vacation. Sometimes when I am very busy at work, I forget to drink enough water.

On other days, e.g., when I don't have that much work to do and when it is cold outside, I find myself drinking a lot of herbal tea to keep me warm.

A typical hydration schedule for me might look like this (one cup is equivalent to eight fl. oz. or 240 ml):

- 1 to 2 cups of water after waking up
- 1 cup of caffeinated tea at breakfast
- 1 to 2 cups of herbal tea in the morning
- One cup after a morning run OR a cup before a pre-lunch run
- 1 to 2 cups of water for lunch
- 1 to 2 cups of herbal tea or water in the afternoon
- 2 cups of water at dinner

During runs over an hour, I would typically drink about 6 to 8 fl. oz. (180 to 240 ml) every 40 minutes with a sports gel (or at least the minimum recommended amount of water for the specific sports gel if that is more) and some extra water when I am thirsty.

I also drink a glass or two of water afterwards OR a post-run recovery drink with protein.

It is worth spending a bit of self-observation to decide on your own philosophy with regards to hydration and rehydration. To give you a place to start, I have pulled together some research to help you to establish your own routine.

REGULAR WATER INTAKE (WITHOUT EXERCISE)

According to the American nonprofit medical center Mayo Clinic, people were healthy if they took in about:

- 15.5 cups (3.7 liters) of fluids (men)
- 11.5 cups (2.7 liters) of fluids a day (women)

Note that this is the amount consumed from all foods and beverages in one day! Your food contains a lot of liquid, especially fruits and vegetables, and provides about 20 % of all the water you need. Therefore, men will likely need to consume no more than 12.4 cups (3 l) per day without exercise, women no more than 9.2 cups (2.2 l).

PRE-RACE HYDRATION

To reach euhydration, an ideal state to exercise in, you will likely need to consume about 2 to 4 ml/lbs (5 to 10 ml/kg) of body weight in the 2 to 4 hours before your race. Avoid drinking too close to your race. Otherwise, you might find yourself standing at the starting line with crossed legs!

HYDRATION DURING THE RACE

Opinions on **prescribed water intake versus ad libitum drinking or drinking to thirst** are in flux right now. Recommendations for race hydration have traditionally been based on the hypothesis that dehydration in excess of 2 % of your body weight leads to decreased performance. This doctrine, however, has been put into question somewhat recently. There seem to be contradicting results on the topic, including from one specific study with half marathon runners.

In lieu of a clearer scientific picture, I can only repeat my personal strategy, which has served me well in the past: **I start drinking (and refueling) early in the race.**

I do not carry additional water with me, but I will drink sports drinks at the refueling stations with the appropriate amount of carbohydrates in them. (More if the weather is hot.) The American College of Sports Medicine's recommendation for "intense prolonged exercise lasting longer than 1 hour" is that athletes should consume between 30 and 60 g of carbohydrates per hour.

RE-HYDRATION AFTER THE RACE

It is often said that you should drink enough after the race **to replace the fluids you have lost.** One indication of how much water you may have lost is to measure your body weight before and after the race. The difference is approximately the amount of water you have shed.

I usually drink 1 to 2 glasses of water or a post-run recovery drink with protein.

CAFFEINE

For a long time, **coffee and tea** were suspected of dehydrating your body, but this has been disproven. If you drink **no more than 180 mg of caffeine** per day, you should be fine. According to the U.S. Food and Drug Administration (FDA), an 8 oz (240 ml) cup of coffee contains about 80 to 100 mg of caffeine; a cup of green or black tea about 30 to 50 mg, and a 12 oz (350 ml) can of caffeinated soda drink roughly 30 to 40 mg. Energy drinks can be much stronger, with up to 250 mg per 8 fl. oz (240 ml)!

I would generally stay away from energy drinks that are not developed for sports. **Sports drinks are generally designed to support your muscle glycogen replenishment, while energy drinks may contain a lot of caffeine and other stimulants and additives that aren't particularly supportive of your body's repair and replenishment.**

In summary:

- For a long time now, the risks of dehydration have been well-known. Overhydrating, exercise-associated hyponatremia (EAH), or "water intoxication" can also be dangerous, though.
- For an ideal state to exercise in (called **euhydration**), you will likely need to consume between **2 to 4 ml/ lbs (5-10 ml/kg) of body weight in the 2 to 4 hours** before your race.

CARB LOADING AND RACE-DAY FUELING

WHAT IS CARB LOADING AND WHY DO IT?

Your brain, muscles, and nerves need **glycogen** to function. When you're running, it's glycogen that provides you with the quick, easy energy you need for top performance. If you run out of glycogen, you'll hit "**the wall**" (also referred to as "**bonking**"): You will feel fatigued and unable to go any further. Since your brain at this point gets as energy-deprived as your muscles, you will also feel weak and unable to concentrate, perhaps even dizzy and nauseous. Ask anybody who has experienced hitting the wall—it's not pretty!

Glycogen, mostly, comes from carbohydrates. All carbs that aren't used immediately are turned into glycogen and stored in your muscles and liver. The idea behind carb loading, therefore, is to make sure your **glycogen stores** are filled to the brim when you start your race.

CARB LOADING STRATEGY

When you carb load, you switch to eating a very **high**

carb diet in the days before the race. This helps fill your glycogen stores.

As mentioned before, I am a certified nutrition coach, but I don't know your personal medical history. What you will find in this chapter is general guidance that works for most healthy adults. If you have any specific questions or feel that the guidance set forth in this chapter will not be appropriate for your specific needs, you should definitely consult a doctor or registered dietitian nutritionist (RDN) to discuss your specific situation. Keep in mind that every person is different and that the general guidelines may not work for you.

If your race is **longer than 75 minutes**—which it presumably will be—you should consume 10 to 12 grams per kilogram of your body weight per 24-hour period, **starting about 48 hours before the race**.

Pick your favorite from the foods below or other **high-carb, low-fat, low-fiber foods**.

(Be careful, though, if you have special dietary requirements, for instance due to diabetes. Carb loading may not be for you, or at least you will have to adjust it to your individual diet and health regime. Do consult your doctor or a registered dietician to discuss how you can best prepare for the race.)

The Mayo Clinic suggests to **carb load on foods such as**:

- plain bagels
- honey
- bananas
- crunchy cereal
- grape juice

- reduced-fat chocolate milk
- blueberries
- unsweetened cranberry juice
- cranberries
- strawberries

If you like, you can try the Mayo Clinic's carb loading meal plan (see reference section). If needed, simply adjust it to your preferences and whatever is readily available to you.

Note that you don't have to eat more. Just make sure that your meals building up to the race contain more carbohydrates than usual.

You want to be careful to eat **low-fiber foods** during carb loading. If not, you risk **gastrointestinal issues** such as bloating or loose stool that might make you feel very uncomfortable during the race. As examples, you may want to skip foods such as broccoli and legumes, since they may cause bloating. Make sure you establish a good routine, ingesting what fuels you well and doesn't cause you any discomfort.

Important: Make sure you test your carb loading strategy! I can't stress this point enough. You don't want to leave it to three days before the race to find out that your strategy is going to make your race day VERY unpleasant! Diarrhea, gas, or flatulence are among the unpleasant side effects that can occur, especially if you are not used to consuming so many carbs at once.

I suggest **starting to test your carb load strategy** on your long runs **3 to 4 weeks before your race**. If you feel confident, then you are probably good to go, and if it did not work out, you still have enough time to come up with other strategies. **Don't underestimate the positive or negative effects your fueling can have on your well-being and your performance!**

Here's what my plan looks like for my carb loading days. (Keep in mind that what worked for me as a woman in my mid-thirties who had just started running again might not work for you.)

Breakfast
one whole bagel
two tablespoons of honey
carb loader drink (by recipe)

Snack
banana

Lunch
4 ½ oz spelt pasta
½ cup marinara sauce
two medium raw carrots
carb load drink (by recipe)

Snack
¼ cup dried cranberries
12 fl. oz grape juice

Dinner
4 ½ oz spelt pasta
½ cup marinara sauce

As you can see, I use a **carb loader drink**. This is a bit unusual and in no way necessary if you don't want to. In fact, I'm only using the product because I'm struggling to ingest enough food in a small amount of time. If this is not a problem for you, it's absolutely perfect to carb load on lots of yummy food!

There are some downsides to carb loader products, too—after all, they do constitute a highly processed artificial kind of "food." If you want to use any such product, it's worth doing some research. Make sure, as with all your nutritional supplements, that it's produced as naturally as possible. Also, be aware that some sports gels, electrolytes, and carb loader products contain **banned substances**. You don't want to become guilty of illegal doping! You can usually find carb loader products in nutrition or vitamin stores or possibly some running stores.

Note also that I'm eating **spelt pasta**. This can be easier to digest than regular pasta.

During the carb loading period, I also eat **white bread** with honey for breakfast (I usually skip the butter) instead of my usual muesli or oatmeal, which are high in **fiber**.

RACE FUELING STRATEGY

You have spent months training for your race. You want the cherry on top. Your fueling on race day can make the difference between an exhilarating experience and swearing to yourself you'll never run a half marathon again, or, worse, bailing on your race. **Much of your race depends upon how well you fueled up before the race and how well you fuel on race day.**

In this section, I am going to walk you through your race-day fueling and help you build a strategy to make your race awesome!

CARBS, CARBS, CARBS BEFORE THE RACE

In the 1 to 4 hours before the race, you will want to consume 1 to 4 grams of carbs per kilogram of your body weight as your pre-event fuel. Make sure your pre-race meal is light, easy to digest, and low in fiber, protein, and fat.

A good, light pre-race meal could be one of the following:

- half a bagel with jelly or honey
- a bowl of white rice
- a high-carb energy bar

CARBS AND ELECTROLYTES DURING THE RACE

To reach your top performance and feel well during the race, you'll also need to consume carbs during the race. **30 to 60 g of carbohydrates per hour** is a good rule of thumb.

Start in the first hour, *before* you run out of fuel!

At many official races, the organizers will provide fueling (e.g., bananas, energy gels, isotonic beverages, or sports bars) at the refueling stations. However, the position of the stations and what they offer varies from race to race. I highly recommend doing some **diligent research** to prepare.

To put together your **fueling plan**, you will need to **check what foods they offer at each of the refueling stations**. Then you need to **calculate** how much you will need to consume, as the amount of carbohydrates can vary by drink or energy bar.

If you plan to use the drinks, gels, or bars they provide at the race, you should definitely **test these specific products beforehand, repeatedly**. Some people don't react well to certain products. If this is the case for you, you might decide to bring your own or have someone carry them for you on the sidelines.

I usually have a gel every 40 minutes with about 4 to 8 fl. oz (180 to 240 ml) of water (starting to count from the beginning of the race, so the first one is at approximately 40 minutes into the race). This way, I consume water and carbohydrates at the same time, which is great.

I bring the gels with me so that I know the exact dosage of carbs.

I usually also take some water from one of the refueling stations. I don't carry water with me, so I try to **time the gels when I reach a water station**. (I don't suggest taking the gels without water. Most of them are advised to be consumed with water; otherwise, they can upset your stomach. It's important to check the instructions on the packaging to ensure you are taking in the fuel in the correct intervals and with the right amount of water.)

CARBS AND PROTEIN AFTER THE RACE

Don't skip refueling after the race! Not only do you need it to refill your energy stores, but it will help your body to repair the tiny fractures in your muscles that you've incurred during the race and to uphold the training effect of your run. **Proper refueling is, in fact, part of your preparation for the next race.** It will help you to recover faster and to avoid injuries in the long run.

In addition to carbohydrates, you need some protein after your run. Often, what you ingest post your race will be a mix of protein and carbohydrates, and this combination has in fact proven to be beneficial. According to the aforementioned Joint Position Statement of the American College of Sports Medicine, **athletes who consumed 0.8 g carbs/kg and 0.4 g proteins/kg were able to replete their glycogen stores as fast as athletes who consumed 1.2 g carbs/kg without proteins**.

In summary:

- For optimal performance during the race, you want to fill your glycogen stores to the brim before the race.
- Start your previously tested carb loading about 48 hours before the race, taking in about **10 to 12 grams per kilogram of your body weight per 24-hour period. Choose high-carb, low-fat, low-fiber foods**.
- During the race, **consume 30 to 60 g of carbohydrates per hour, starting in the first hour**.

MENTAL GAME

"I'm not running with my legs alone. I'm running with my heart and my mind." That's what the fastest marathoner on earth, Eliud Kipchoge, says about his unmatched performance. He is the first person to run a marathon in under two hours, and he predicted his groundbreaking 2019 achievement with absolute confidence: he was sure he was going to make history and pave the way for others who would follow him.

Many of the world's leading athletes have repeated over and over what Eliud is hinting at: it's all about the mental game. Even the most disciplined training, the fanciest equipment, and the best preparation will not get you anywhere unless you acquire the necessary psychological strength that is needed for a long-distance run such as a half marathon.

When I was writing this book, I asked over 100 runners what their biggest challenge was in training for a half marathon. Many said the mental game. Often, their fears revolved around not being able to cover the distance. Some feel the same anxiety for their long training runs.

I know exactly what they mean. Once I had all the physical preparation handled and concentrated on the mental game, everything became much easier. I felt much more confident and was less anxious that I might fail.

MENTAL PREPARATION

There are eight areas of mental preparation: consistency; planning; visualization; having a backup plan; turning nervousness into excitement; building on your successes and learning from your failures; celebrating the small things; and remembering your WHY.

Consistency

Some people like very structured routines and find it easy to stick with them. Others, like me, cringe at the concept. They feel that it takes away their freedom and spontaneity. I only learned the value of **reliable, regular routines** after my son was born, and I had to juggle all the extra responsibilities and tasks. Once I applied this life lesson and introduced a constant routine into my running (i.e., doing my running at the same time on the same weekdays), I was finally able to complete most workouts as planned. **I overcame procrastination and stopped skipping workouts.** Because every run had its **predictable place within my daily and weekly schedules**, I could consistently prepare for my runs and get my gear ready the evening before. That way, going on a run **took a lot less discipline** than making brand-new decisions every day—I just did what I was scheduled to do whenever I was supposed to do it. **With my new habit, my workout completion rate increased drastically.**

Going against my natural impulses and instead favoring a strict routine had other beneficial side effects, too. For instance, **I got my sleeping habits under control.** How did that happen? Well, I had difficulty squeezing in my runs over lunch or in the evening. During the day, there were too many excuses to not do my workouts, and in the evening, after a long day of work, I had less control over my willpower. So, I decided I would have to complete my runs in the morning right after my son had left for school and before I went to work.

Now, I don't know about you, but I am not a morning person. So, the thought of early-morning runs seemed daunting at first. But it forced me to go to bed on time and wake up at the same time every morning, even on weekends. Since I changed my routine, I am much more consistent with my training and my sleeping/waking rhythm, and I feel awesome—physically and mentally. A surprisingly easy pro tip to establish consistency and routines: lay out your running clothes and gear the day before. That way, you are dressed and ready before you know it, and your shoes will almost walk you out the door on their own!

Planning

Another potential hurdle to get out of the way before your run is **to plan out your route and your metrics** (see Training chapter). The more uncertainties you remove, the more you can focus on your mental game. Most training plans will dictate what zone you will run in for the different segments of the workout. I made it a point to decide ahead of time **exactly** what speed or wattage to run on which part of my route. This left no room for interpretation and allowed me to stay focused.

Also, it's good to know exactly what metrics you want to apply for your success. An accomplished ultra-runner once said to me, "You know, I may not be fast, but I am happy to run along at 10:00 min/mi for a very long time." That made me realize one of the criteria for success that I had not met yet: I sometimes stopped running and started walking because I found it hard to stay focused. And that bothered me. My goal for the race was to keep running for the whole duration.

At that time, I was preparing for my 2019 half marathon. I had not run a half marathon in more than two years, and I had had a couple of disastrous long runs, particularly my longest run.

As I was mentally preparing for the race the evening before, I decided that if I got the urge to walk during the race, I would slow down my pace to a comfortable level for half a mile. By slowing down, I was taking some of the mental pressure off, which allowed me to keep running, refocus, and pick up the pace again later. I was pretty excited when I ran the entire race (except for a few steps of walking at the rehydration stations).

If you can figure out your mental game challenges ahead of time and develop a plan on how you are going to deal with them, you will be prepared to cope with them.

Visualization

This technique might be THE most powerful skill that distinguishes successful athletes from the rest of the pack. Eliud Kipchoge, when asked how he visualized his famous run in Vienna, answered, "I have visualized [it] in my heart; I have put [it] in my mind; and what I think will happen is that I will break the two-hour barrier."

Here's how I do it: Before a long run, I spend a couple of minutes visualizing the route, the sensation of running and what it will feel like when the going gets tough. I emulate how I will cope with the challenges that will undoubtedly arise. This practice allows me to approach my runs with more confidence.

In areas where you have run frequently, you probably roughly remember where there will be birds chirping, what the air will smell like on different parts of the path, or how cool or warm it will be. These are all part of the visualization.

One of my runs leads me along a busy road until it veers off into a greener area, through a short piece of forest, over a bridge with a steep approach, and then through some fields where the air is always much warmer.

When I visualize this run, I imagine how I run the opposite direction of the cars, how I can hear the cars, smell the gasoline, and feel the whizzing of the air when a bus goes by. As I imagine running through the forest, I can feel the coolness of the shade, and I can smell the pine trees. As I visualize the steep approach to the bridge, I feel my legs burning up the hill. As I come down to the fields, I sense that warmer air heating up my body, and I start telling myself: **go, go, go, Bev**. This is the corner where I would typically have tried to wiggle out of my run before because it felt uncomfortable to run through these warm fields in the summer. Now that I visualize my runs, I am prepared to stick it out.

If I have never run in the area where I am going to run, I try to figure out from the **Google Maps** topology what the different areas could look and feel like and prepare my mind for something new. I decide beforehand that I will just take in the new surroundings and be curious what is out there. **I also prepare myself for what to do if I feel like stopping.** One strategy that works for me is to tell myself that I am going to run slower.

Having a Backup Plan

On some days, you will be in top form, and on other days, you might not feel quite as strong. It's good to think of a contingency plan on any given day.

I used to have one workout on my training schedule that I dreaded so much that I developed some type of mental block to it. It was the one that had me going from zone one to two and then ending in zone three. I found this so painful to do, I frequently gave up. I would always find an excuse not to do it.

If you are afraid of a run, you start seeing it as something really undesirable—which takes away all the joy of working towards your bigger goal.

The way I solved this problem was to set out to do the full workout as planned, but to allow myself to drop to zone two or, worst-case, zone one if I was not able to sustain zone three. This way, firstly, I would still cover the whole distance even if I did not complete the workout exactly as planned. Secondly, and even more importantly, I could file the experience away as a success instead of as a failure, which raised my confidence. As time went by, I started completing them as they were on the training plan. That way, I ended up on an even better track with my training.

So if you are preparing for a race or training run, come prepared with a contingency plan to make sure you can log your experience as a success.

Turning Nervousness into Excitement

No matter how well you prepare and how much confidence you have in your training, you might still get nervous when you run a race. It can happen to everybody, including top athletes. But the best of the best don't say they're nervous. Instead, they say, "**I'm excited.**"

Excitement and nervousness are both high-energy emotions. But excitement is a positive one. And changing your mindset from a negative to a positive emotion can impact your performance. You start looking at what's ahead of you **as an opportunity, rather than a threat**.

Researchers at Harvard Business School have studied this phenomenon in detail, and Simon Sinek talks about it often, as well. I learned the lesson from public speaking and am applying it to any challenging situation, including a race: when I start to get nervous, I tell everybody that I am excited. **When someone asks me if I am nervous, I say, "No, I am excited!"** Also, I imagine myself having fun during the race, enjoying the competition, the crowds cheering, the bands playing on the final stretch …

In short: I channel my emotion into excitement. And excitement and confidence combined make a winning duo!

Building on Your Successes,
Learning from Your Failures

When I mentally prepare for a race or a long run, I think back to all the positive experiences I have had during my preparation up until that stage. In most training plans, the long runs build up from week to week. This means that each week you run a bit farther, usually without any problem. **Knowing that you have successfully completed all these strenuous workouts** gives you the confidence that you can handle the one ahead of you.

If negative self-talk creeps in, I concentrate on my learnings from negative experiences and ensure that all potential hurdles have been removed. This time, it is going to be different because you prepared! For instance: In the beginning, I bonked or dried out on more runs than I wish to remember. Now, I know how to fuel adequately, water- and calorie-wise, so it won't happen again.

Celebrating the Small Things in Life

My family has gotten into the habit of celebrating the small things in life. We keep half bottles of champagne in the fridge so that we can grab one whenever we have something to celebrate. (And if we don't feel like drinking alcohol, homemade juice cocktails or alcohol-free beer are our go-to fun alternatives). **We celebrate effort, not only achievement.**

That includes completing a half marathon—no matter if the target time was met or not. We also celebrate the **milestones** along the way: if you complete a preparatory

10k, that is a reason to celebrate. If you are a first-time runner, you can even celebrate your first week of training. **Keep on celebrating!** It's fun and motivating.

Remembering Your WHY

At the beginning of this book, we started by finding our **WHY**. When you are out there suffering and perhaps struggling on your run, that's the perfect time to remember your WHY. Why are you out here running? Is it because you want to bring home a certificate saying you ran a sub two-hour half marathon? Is it because you want to lose weight, raise a certain amount of money for charity, or simply feel fitter? **Bringing your WHY back to life can help you push through all barriers.**

What I always like to do in these mental battles is to remember my WHY. That's why I came up with it in the first place! The one time I try to bring my WHY back into the forefront of my conscience is when I am faced with going on a run now or later—in other words procrastinating getting out of the house.

When I remember that I usually feel pretty awesome after a run, I can overcome the resistance of getting out into the snowy, dark morning or evening and start moving down the road. Getting back home then once again confirms that amazing feeling and strengthens how I feel about my WHY—particularly for the next time.

In summary:

- Even if you are not usually the type for it, establishing a good training routine will make all the difference. As the saying goes: First, you make your habits; then the habits make you. That includes systematic **mental preparation**, too. If you know how to handle your personal, unique distractions, challenges, or excuses, they cannot interfere with your training or race.
- The following are all good ways to strengthen your mental power as a runner:
  - consistency
  - planning
  - visualization
  - building on your successes and learning from your failures
  - having a backup plan
  - turning nervousness into excitement
  - celebrating the small things in life
  - remembering your WHY

ACE YOUR RACE

You are almost there! Soon, you are going to run YOUR race! You should be proud of yourself. By the time you make it to the start line, you will have anywhere from of 12 to 24 weeks of training under your belt, depending on what stage you started at as a runner.

Doing the final preparations for the race is super exciting! All your training and careful preparation will now culminate in that ever-so-energizing and joy-filled moment of completing your first half marathon!

Remember when we talked about your **mental game**? As you get closer, some people might start to ask you if you are ready or if you are nervous. **You are not nervous. You are EXCITED!**

Now, hold your horses. Don't sprint out the gate just yet… You'll need to contain your enthusiasm at least a bit to be able to make it through the race gracefully and not crawl across the finish line on all fours.

Much of the success of your race day lies in careful preparation in the last month before the race. You'll want to get your fueling, race equipment, race pacing, and race-day details sorted out during these final weeks.

In this chapter, you will find **detailed checklists** of what to prepare to be ready on the big day.

FOUR WEEKS BEFORE THE RACE

By the month before the race, **you will have already done a lot of the heavy lifting**. You will now be doing your **longest runs**, and you might start to feel the fatigue of all your hard work in your body. During this last phase, make sure you are particularly vigilant to act immediately if you think you feel an **injury** coming on. Make sure you **avoid getting any colds or other bugs**. (Don't eat from the same plates or lick your kids' spoon, wash your hands frequently, etc. It's happened to me more than once that I managed to catch a cold from my young son in the last days before the race and couldn't run.)

And **don't be too tough on yourself**. If you need to take a day off because you are feeling too tired, it's okay. Do it. I give you permission! You're going to be all right.

At about four weeks before your half marathon, you'll want to do a **10k prep race**. There are three good reasons to do this. One, it gives you the **experience of getting all your gear, fueling, and race logistics in order**.

Secondly, you want to use this race time to help **predict your half marathon race time**. I suggest you run your 10k at an organized race, if possible, but of course you can also do it virtually or on your own. One crucial point is that you should **avoid running your 10k in a recovery week** since it will be a hard effort. Recovery weeks are weeks where your long run and mileage for the week are less than the previous weeks and should not include any strenuous efforts such as all out races.

Thirdly, the 10k race allows you to **test your equipment for the race**. For example, if you are going to be using different shoes for your race, you can try them here. (You don't want to wear them for the first time at the race and find out that they give you blisters!)

You should also **test any special functions on your watch or apps** which you might want to use during the race. On that note: I once went into a half marathon race with a new watch and realized that when I put it in running mode, I didn't have a distance on any of the screens because I had been training by time! I had no clue what mile in the race I was on! Even worse, I had decided to lap my watch at the 10k, which I had never done in training, and found out that my watch skipped to the next mile! When I did get a mile completion summary screen, it was not even the correct mile marker. All I could say to myself was ARGGHH! And it was annoying for the whole race.

If the climate at your 10k is similar to that of the race destination, you will likely want to test as much of your **clothing and equipment**, including undergarments and accessories such as hats, gloves or sunglasses, etc., as you can.

Here's a list of what you might want to test during your 10k race:

- ❑ running clothes: shirt, shorts/leggings/pants, jackets
- ❑ shoes
- ❑ socks
- ❑ undergarments: underwear, bra (for the ladies)
- ❑ fuel belt for your nutrition
- ❑ water or electrolyte bottles, or hydration packs
- ❑ hat/sun visor/sunglasses

- ❑ gloves
- ❑ training watch/app
- ❑ sunscreen
- ❑ any nutrition such as gels, etc.

In the months before your race, you'll also want to **start testing your fueling strategy on your long runs**. (This would be a good time to review the Carb Loading and Race Day Fueling chapter and decide what nutrition you want to consume at what point in your long runs and race.)

If you are going to carb load, this is the phase in which you will want to try the strategy. I suggest starting your **carb load strategy testing** at least four weeks before your race to ensure you don't do it on your last long run—just in case you need to adjust your fueling strategy.

Fueling to some degree is highly individual and will take some tweaking. You will probably be refining your fueling strategy for years to come as a runner, but you want to give yourself at least a bit of leeway to try a couple of different approaches before your first race.

TWO WEEKS BEFORE THE RACE

You are now approaching **your longest run. Take it with ease, relax, and enjoy it.** If it doesn't work out perfectly, **DON'T** try to redo it! Just put it behind you and don't worry about it. You are going to be fine—you have done a great job in preparing. You have done a lot of good hard work, and **you have prepared yourself mentally for**

the most likely challenges that might creep up on you
during the race (see Mental Game). It is vital in the two
weeks before the race that you let your body recover and
ease up your training load.

This is called **tapering**. It means you will be reducing
your training load so that your body can recover enough
to be in **peak** running form on the day of the race. When
your body reaches optimal race condition, we call that
"peaking." (If you ever skipped a few workouts during
training, you might have seen that status before on your
training watch as well.)

Now is also the time to review the **details of the race
and the logistics** of getting yourself to the right place at
the right time.

Here's a checklist of what you'll want to check on:

❑ Check the exact location and print a map of the
following:
  ○ where you will pick up your start number
  ○ where the race will start and finish
  ○ where your changing room is located
  ○ where the bathrooms are located
  ○ where valuables can be deposited
❑ Check the latest time to pick up your start number
(sometimes they are sent to your home; ensure you
received it)
❑ Organize transportation to the event location,
ensuring you have enough time to pick up your start
number, change, deposit valuables, and warm up
❑ Review your race route and altitude profile along the

route. This will help you anticipate what comes next during your races, especially when you are tired

❑ Tell all your fans about the race and invite them to come and cheer you on

Two weeks before the race is also the ideal time to start thinking about your race strategy.

Race Strategy and Race Pacing

One of the critical points to pace your half marathon well is not to go out too fast. With all the excitement of the race, the music, the other people running with you, and, of course, the adrenaline rush you get from hearing the start gun, it's super easy to go out way too fast—and you'll feel good for a while until reality sets in. It will likely catch up with you later in the race, and it could be pretty painful.

Ideally, the second half of your race will be faster than the first half. If there is only one thing you remember about pacing on the day, then make it this: no matter how good you feel, go out about 5 to 15 s/mi (3 to 10 s/km) slower than your desired race pace on the first one to two miles. This will help you from burning yourself out on the second half of the race.

If you did a 10k race or time trial, you will want to use that to predict your approximate time for your race. (Keep in mind that you will have to adjust your timing if you are running a hilly course.)

No worries if you did not run a 10k in the month before the race; there are other ways to predict your race pace.

I recommend using McMillan's Free Running Calculator at https://www.mcmillanrunning.com/. (You will find instructions on the page on how to use the calculator.)

Some races also offer **pacers**. These are runners who volunteer to run the course at a specific pace to achieve a certain finish time. The beauty about running with a pacer is that you only need to focus on one thing: sticking to the pacer. Everything else is their job!

If there are no pacers, make sure you line up in your start block with people that will run approximately your pace. Keep in mind that many people, particularly the less experienced runners, tend to go out too fast. If you find that everyone goes out faster than you do, don't allow yourself to be tempted. Just **stick to your plan**. Tell yourself that you will be rewarded later while they might get a nasty payback.

2 TO 3 DAYS BEFORE THE RACE

At the 2 to 3 day mark before the race, you will want to **start preparing for your carb loading**, if you plan to do that (see Carb Loading chapter). This would also be a good point in time to **review your race-day fueling strategy for pre-, during, and post-race** (see Fueling and Refueling chapter).

Make sure you have all the right foods in the house to execute your fueling and hydration strategies for pre-, during, and post-race. This is also an excellent time to remind your fans that you will be racing. Depending on how many people will come and watch, you might want them to meet you at different spots on the race to cheer you on.

This is also the ideal point in time to **start preparing your pre- and post-race bag**. Make sure all your equipment is in order and that your favorite race clothes are clean and ready. You don't want to have to make a mad dash out the house for any gels you forgot to buy or any other equipment that is not in order.

Check the race-day checklist in the next section to ensure you have everything ready to be packed the night before.

THE DAY BEFORE THE RACE

You're almost there! It's the day before the race—time to relax. Enjoy your evening with an early night of quality sleep. This is not the day for wild parties or late bedtime! You want to prepare yourself to be in top form on race day—physically as well as mentally—for which sleep is critical.

Make sure your bag is packed for race day and do all your **final logistics checks**. Watch a motivating movie or prepare any **race-day music** you want to take along.

Race-day Prep Checklist

❑ check the weather
❑ charge all your devices that you will need, e.g., your training watch, music player, etc.
❑ confirm your ride or departure time for your means of transport

❑ ensure your tickets are packed if you already purchased them

❑ confirm the parking location if you plan to drive

❑ reserve any ground transportation to get you to your race destination

❑ confirm your hotel reservation and location if you are traveling the night before the race

❑ set all your alarms to wake up in time. Set multiples, just to be sure.

Equipment Checklist

❑ directions to start line

❑ race number & timing chip

❑ four safety pins for the race number

❑ racing shoes

❑ socks

❑ t-shirt, plus jacket (if necessary)

❑ shorts/pants/leggings

❑ undergarments: underwear, bra (for the ladies)

❑ tracksuit to warm up if necessary

❑ fuel belt

❑ hydration pack/water bottle

❑ nutrition

❑ headphones

❑ music player

❑ training watch

❑ hat/visor

❑ gloves (depending on weather)

❑ sunglasses

- ❏ sunscreen
- ❏ anti-chafe cream/gel (if desired)
- ❏ chargers for all your devices

Post-race bag:

- ❏ sandals or shoes for after the race
- ❏ fresh clothes and undergarments
- ❏ cash for after-race snack or meal
- ❏ recovery drink
- ❏ recovery foods
- ❏ shower gel
- ❏ towel
- ❏ band-aids

THE DAY OF THE RACE

You made it. Today's the day! And remember, you are EXCITED! You are pumped and ready to ace that race! Close your eyes, take a deep breath, and visualize how you are going to hear the start gun, how you are going to go out a little slower than your target race pace, perhaps a little slower than the other runners. You are going to cruise the 13.1 mi (21.1 km) and cross the finish line with a smile and two thumbs up! It's going to be great. All your hard work and preparation will pay off. AND don't forget to smile at all the cameras along the way. That's going to be THE most important part—having the memories to prove you did it!

If you are racing in the morning, **being up four hours before the race** will allow your body to be alert and ready to run. The half marathon will require the freshest legs you can offer. This means that if your race is in the evening, make sure you stay off your feet as much as you can during the day.

In some event locations, the point where you pick up your number, the changing rooms, and the valuables deposit can be quite far apart. Try to find the most efficient route between these points to avoid excessive walking before your race. (This usually means avoiding the fair at the race until after the race.) To feel as relaxed as possible, give yourself plenty of time to find the changing rooms and to prepare for the race.

Race-day Preparation Checklist

❑ light race-day breakfast
❑ light nutrition before the race
❑ pick up your race number
❑ deposit your valuables
❑ change for the race (don't forget to pin on your race number and put on your timing chip!)
❑ review your race strategy
❑ review your fueling strategy
❑ prepare your race nutrition and fill your water/electrolyte bottles
❑ warm-up
❑ last bathroom visit—line up in time! Lines can get long right before the race
❑ line up in your starting block

- ❑ find your pacer if you are following one
- ❑ RUN!!! But DON'T start too fast! Remember to stay relaxed when you start and go out slower than you plan to finish

AFTER THE RACE

Congratulations, you did it! **This is a remarkable achievement!** You should enjoy all your efforts, celebrate, and pat yourself on the back for having raced your first half marathon!

You have been very diligent about your nutrition leading up to the race. Now it's time to party and have some fun. (Don't go too crazy on the alcohol, though, particularly if you are dehydrated.)

After the race (and your victory celebration), you will need some time to recover from your great efforts. Your training plan might tell you what to do for recovery, or you might have purchased a two-week recovery plan. If not, the easiest recovery method is to do **reverse training**. In other words, you do the last week of your training plan, and then the second-to-last week of your training plan. Check the Carb Loading and Race Day Fueling chapter on what to eat and drink after the race. This will allow you to be in prime condition again to run your next race soon.

In summary:

- Four weeks before the race, you will start running your longest runs. If you can, participate in a 10k run now to get some racing experience and to test your equipment, fueling strategy, and mental game.
- Two weeks before the race, you will start tapering, which means you will reduce your training load to allow your body time to recover and get into peak performance state. This is a good time to prepare your racing strategy. Probably the most important thing is not to start too fast: go out about 5 to 15 s/mi (3 to 10s/km) slower than your desired race pace on the first one to two miles. Your goal is for the second half of your race being faster than the first half.
- 2 to 3 days before the race, you should start carb loading, if you have decided to do it. This is the time to prepare your pre-, during, and post-race fueling strategy too.
- On race day, be prepared to have a light pre-race break-fast in time and some light pre-race nutrition (high carb, low fat, no fiber!) before the race.
- After the race is before the next race! With the right recovery training, you will be excellently prepared to run your next half marathon soon! Recovery train with your training plan (if it entails post-race recovery), using a specific two-week recovery training plan, or by simply reversing the last and second-to-last weeks of your half marathon training plan.

WELL DONE! You have officially become a HALF MARATHON RUNNER! Welcome to the club. It has been a pleasure guiding you through your half marathon preparation. I can only hope that you will stick with running and get as much pleasure out of it as I do!

I was a serious running athlete for 13 years, and then I stopped being one for 13 years. Now, I've become a half marathon runner, and I will keep running for the rest of my life. How can I be so sure? Because it makes me healthy and happy and alert. Because it keeps my body and my brain in perfect shape. Because it gives me joy, inspiration, and beautiful experiences in nature. Because it challenges me in exactly the way I want.

How about you? When will you run your next half marathon? Once again: welcome to the world of running!

ACKNOWLEDGMENTS

My warmest, massive thanks go out to the following people without whom this book would not exist: first and foremost, to my readers, the reason I wrote the book in the first place!

Huge thanks to my husband, Florian, who endured many reads of the book and kept me going.

And to my best friend Paz, who was always there to discuss all my crazy ideas with me and who gently guided me towards feeling like a proper author—thank you!

A massively warm thanks to my father, John, who read several versions of the book and was my greatest cheerleader along the way.

And to my mother, Erika, who was always there to listen and pick me back up every time I had gotten off track.

A big shout-out to my incredibly fantastic content editor Sonja, who breathed life into this book.

Great thanks also to all my beta readers: Thomas, Isabelle, Caroline, Sarah, Tatyana. Your feedback was super valuable and motivating.

The book's roots—thanks to the Global Corporate Challenge team that got me running again: Thomas G., Thomas L., Thomas D., Alex, Bruno, and Ralf.

And, of course, many thanks to Morgan and the Paper Raven Books team for helping me bring my book out to the world.

REFERENCES & FURTHER READING

MY LIFE AS A RUNNER

1. Virgin Pulse Global Challenge. n.d. Accessed Dec. 9, 2021. https://www.virginpulse.com/vp-go/.

WHY RUNNING IS GOOD FOR YOU

1. Chika Anekwe, MD, MPH. May 17, 2021. "More movement, better memory." Harvard Health Publishing. https://www.health.harvard.edu/blog/more-movement-better-memory-202105172457.
2. David J. Linden, Ph.D. n.d. Accessed Dec. 9, 2021. "The Truth Behind 'Runner's High' and Other Mental Benefits of Running." Johns Hopkins Medicine. https://www.hopkinsmedicine.org/health/wellness-and-prevention/the-truth-behind-runners-high-and-other-mental-benefits-of-running.
3. "Exercising for Better Sleep." n.d. Accessed Dec. 9, 2021. Johns Hopkins Medicine. https://www.

hopkinsmedicine.org/health/wellness-and-prevention/
exercising-for-better-sleep.

4. "Physical activity." Nov. 26, 2020. World Health
   Organization. https://www.who.int/news-room/
   fact-sheets/detail/physical-activity.

5. Reynolds, Gretchen. Mar. 10, 2020. "How Exercise
   May Affect Your Immunity." New York Times.

6. "Spending time outdoors is good for you,
   from the Harvard Health Letter." Jul. 1,
   2010. Harvard Health Publisher. https://
   www.health.harvard.edu/press_releases/
   spending-time-outdoors-is-good-for-you.

7. "The Effects of Poor Sleep in the Workplace."
   n.d. Accessed Dec. 9, 2021. Wellness Council of America. https://www.welcoa.org/blog/
   effects-poor-sleep-workplace/.

8. WHO guidelines on physical activity and sedentary
   behaviour. 2020. World Health Organization.

EQUIPMENT

1. Triola, Paige. Jun. 14, 2021. "How Long Do
   Running Shoes Last?". Runner's World. https://
   www.runnersworld.com/gear/a33233314/
   how-many-miles-do-running-shoes-last/.

TRAINING

1. "80/20 Endurance Training Plans." n.d. Accessed Dec. 9, 2021. https://www.8020endurance.com/plans/run-plans/.
2. Alger, Kieran. Sep. 29, 2018. "What is 'running to power' and how can it help your pacing problems?". Runner's World. https://www.runnersworld.com/uk/training/a776426/what-is-running-power/.
3. "Beginner's Half Marathon Plan." Aug. 17, 2015. Runner's World. https://www.runnersworld.com/training/a20831650/beginners-half-marathon-plan-0/.
4. "Couch to 5k Training App." n.d. Accessed Dec. 9, 2021. http://www.c25kfree.com/.
5. Final Surge. n.d. Accessed Dec. 9, 2021. https://www.finalsurge.com/.
6. "Hal Higdon Half Marathon Training Plans." n.d. Accessed Dec. 9, 2021. https://www.halhigdon.com/training/half-marathon-training/.
7. Ignaszewski, Maya; Lau, Benny; Wong, Shannon; Isserow, Saul. 2017. "The Science of Exercise Prescription: Martti Karvonen and his Contributions." BCMJ 59 (1): 38-41. https://bcmj.org/articles/science-exercise-prescription-martti-karvonen-and-his-contributions.
8. "Intermediate Half Marathon Plan." Aug. 17, 2015. Runner's World. https://www.runnersworld.com/training/a20849910/intermediate-half-marathon-plan-0/.
9. Latter, Philip. Mar. 16, 2016. "Essential guide to long

runs." https://www.runnersworld.com/uk/training/a774616/essential-guide-to-long-runs/.

10. Mateo, Ashley. Oct. 19, 2019. "Slower Recovery Runs Can Help You Speed Up—Here's How." https://www.runnersworld.com/training/a25347729/jogging-a-recovery-run/.

11. Middlebrook, Hailey. Jun. 2, 2020. "How to Build Up Mileage Safely this Summer." Runner's World. https://www.runnersworld.com/advanced/a20838835/increasing-mileage-safely/.

12. "Rated Perceived Exertion (RPE) Scale." Feb. 25, 2019. Cleveland Clinic. https://my.clevelandclinic.org/health/articles/17450-rated-perceived-exertion-rpe-scale.

13. "Run Your Butt Off! Training Plan." Aug. 17, 2015. Runner's World. https://www.runnersworld.com/training/a20819360/run-your-butt-off-training-plan/

14. "The 6 Most Common Running Injuries (Plus How to Treat Them)." Oct. 28, 2020. Cleveland Clinic Health Essentials. https://health.clevelandclinic.org/the-most-common-running-injuries-plus-how-to-treat-them/.

15. Training Peaks. n.d. Accessed Dec. 9, 2021. https://www.trainingpeaks.com/.

16. Wade, Alison. Oct. 10, 2014. "The Most Common Injuries From Too-Quick Mileage Increases." Runner's World. https://www.runnersworld.com/health-injuries/a20823591/the-most-common-injuries-from-too-quick-mileage-increases/.

17.   "What are heart rate zones?". Polar. Nov. 5, 2020. https://www.polar.com/us-en/smart-coaching/what-are-heart-rate-zones.

MOTIVATION

1. Chariots of Fire. 1981. Hugh Hudson. 20th Century Fox. https://www.imdb.com/title/tt0082158/.
2. Great Runs. n.d. Accessed Dec. 9, 2021. https://greatruns.com/.
3. MapMyRun. n.d. Accessed Dec. 9, 2021. https://www.mapmyrun.com/.
4. McMillan, Greg. n.d. Accessed Dec. 9, 2021. "Top 3 Reasons Runners Fail." https://www.mcmillanrunning.com/top-3-reasons-runners-fail/.
5. Rocky Balboa. 2006. Sylvester Stallone. Columbia Pictures, MGM, Revolution Studios. https://www.imdb.com/title/tt0479143.
6. Run Every Day. n.d. Accessed Dec. 9, 2021. https://www.runeveryday.com/.
7. Runner's World. n.d. Accessed Dec. 9, 2021. https://www.runnersworld.com/.
8. Strava. n.d. Accessed Dec. 9, 2021. https://www.strava.com/.
9. Trail Runner. n.d. Accessed Dec. 9, 2021. https://www.trailrunnermag.com/.

FUELING

1. Institute of Medicine (U.S.). Panel on Macronutrients., and Institute of Medicine (U.S.). Standing Committee on the Scientific Evaluation of Dietary Reference Intakes. 2005. Dietary reference intakes for energy, carbohydrate, fiber, fat, fatty acids, cholesterol, protein, and amino acids. Washington, D.C.: National Academies Press.

2. "Listing of vitamins." 2020. Harvard Health Publishing. https://www.health.harvard.edu/staying-healthy/listing_of_vitamins.

3. Mark D Muffin, Sachiko T St Jeor, Lisa A Hill, Barbara J Scott,, and Young O Koh Sandra A Daugherty. 1990. The American Journal of Clinical Nutrition 51: 241-7.

4. McArdle, William D., Frank I. Katch, and Victor L. Katch. 2015. Exercise physiology : nutrition, energy, and human performance. Eighth edition. ed. Philadelphia: Wolters Kluwer Health/Lippincott Williams & Wilkins.

5. "Nutrition rules that will fuel your workout." Feb. 23, 2021. Mayo Clinic. https://www.mayoclinic.org/healthy-lifestyle/nutrition-and-healthy-eating/in-depth/nutrition-rules-that-will-fuel-your-workout/art-20390073.

6. Thomas, D. T., K. A. Erdman, and L. M. Burke. 2016. "American College of Sports Medicine Joint Position Statement. Nutrition and Athletic Performance." Med Sci Sports Exerc 48 (3): 543-68.

https://doi.org/10.1249/MSS.0000000000000852. https://www.ncbi.nlm.nih.gov/pubmed/26891166.

7. MyPlate Plan. n.d. Accessed Dec. 9, 2021. https://www.myplate.gov/myplate-plan.

8. "Trans fat is double trouble for your heart health." Feb. 13, 2020. Mayo Clinic. https://www.mayoclinic.org/diseases-conditions/high-blood-cholesterol/in-depth/trans-fat/art-20046114.

HYDRATION

1. Armstrong, L. E., E. C. Johnson, and M. F. Bergeron. 2016. "COUNTERVIEW: Is Drinking to Thirst Adequate to Appropriately Maintain Hydration Status During Prolonged Endurance Exercise? No." Wilderness Environ Med 27 (2): 195-8. https://doi.org/10.1016/j.wem.2016.03.002. https://www.ncbi.nlm.nih.gov/pubmed/27291700.

2. Frank, Michelle. 2019. "The Neuroscience of Thirst: How your brain tells you to look for water." Harvard University. https://sitn.hms.harvard.edu/flash/2019/neuroscience-thirst-brain-tells-look-water/.

3. Hew-Butler, T., V. Loi, A. Pani, and M. H. Rosner. 2017. "Exercise-Associated Hyponatremia: 2017 Update." Front Med (Lausanne) 4: 21. https://doi.org/10.3389/fmed.2017.00021. https://www.ncbi.nlm.nih.gov/pubmed/28316971.

4. Hoffman, M. D., J. D. Cotter, ÉD Goulet, and P. B.

Laursen. 2016. "VIEW: Is Drinking to Thirst Adequate to Appropriately Maintain Hydration Status During Prolonged Endurance Exercise? Yes." Wilderness Environ Med 27 (2): 192-5. https://doi.org/10.1016/j.wem.2016.03.003. https://www.ncbi.nlm.nih.gov/pubmed/27291699.

5. Noakes, T. D., and D. B. Speedy. 2006. "Case proven: exercise associated hyponatraemia is due to overdrinking. So why did it take 20 years before the original evidence was accepted?" Br J Sports Med 40 (7): 567-72. https://doi.org/10.1136/bjsm.2005.020354. https://www.ncbi.nlm.nih.gov/pubmed/16799109.

6. Orton, Kathy. 2002. "Woman Dies 2 Days After Running in Marine Corps Marathon." The Washington Post. 2002. https://www.washingtonpost.com/archive/sports/2002/10/31/woman-dies-2-days-after-running-in-marine-corps-marathon/5766eb4e-30d4-4321-97e6-efd6cf071e13/.

7. "Runner's Death Blamed on Too Much Fluid." 2002. Los Angeles Times. https://www.latimes.com/archives/la-xpm-2002-aug-14-na-briefs14.1-story.html.

8. "Spilling the Beans: How Much Caffeine is Too Much?". 2018. U.S. Food and Drug Administration (FDA). https://www.fda.gov/consumers/consumer-updates/spilling-beans-how-much-caffeine-too-much.

9. Thomas, D. T., K. A. Erdman, and L. M. Burke. 2016. "American College of Sports Medicine Joint Position Statement. Nutrition and Athletic

Performance." Med Sci Sports Exerc 48 (3): 543-68. https://doi.org/10.1249/MSS.0000000000000852. https://www.ncbi.nlm.nih.gov/pubmed/26891166.

10.	"Water: How much should you drink every day?". 2020. Mayo Clinic. https://www.mayoclinic.org/healthy-lifestyle/nutrition-and-healthy-eating/in-depth/water/art-20044256.

CARB LOADING AND RACE DAY FUELING

1. Thomas, D. T., K. A. Erdman, and L. M. Burke. 2016. "American College of Sports Medicine Joint Position Statement. Nutrition and Athletic Performance." Med Sci Sports Exerc 48 (3): 543-68. https://doi.org/10.1249/MSS.0000000000000852. https://www.ncbi.nlm.nih.gov/pubmed/26891166.

2. Mayo Clinic Staff. Jan. 05, 2021. "Carbohydrate-loading diet". https://www.mayoclinic.org/healthy-lifestyle/nutrition-and-healthy-eating/in-depth/carbohydrate-loading/art-20048518.

MENTAL GAME

1. Brooks, A. W. 2014. "Get excited: reappraising pre-performance anxiety as excitement." J Exp

Psychol Gen 143 (3): 1144-58. https://www.ncbi.nlm.nih.gov/pubmed/24364682.

2. Kipchoge, Eliud. 2017. If you don't rule your mind, your mind will rule you.: Facebook. https://www.facebook.com/watch/?v=563070734029832.

3. Sinek, Simon. 2018. Nervous vs. Excited. YouTube. https://www.youtube.com/watch?v=0SUTInEaQ3Q.